SERIOUS
ABOUT
RETIRING

SERIOUS ABOUT RETIRING

A Practical Roadmap for a Healthier, Wealthier, Happier Retirement

Mark S. Fischer
CFP™ & MBA

TEMUNA PRESS
Minneapolis 2019

ISBN: 978-1-7335091-0-7
Library of Congress Control Number: 2018914674

9 8 7 6 5 4 3 2 1
First Edition

Printed in the United States of America

Cover and Interior Design: Sarah Miner
Author photo: Sid Konikoff
Drawings: Lucy Rose Fischer
Publication management: Rachel Holscher
Published by Temuna Press, Minneapolis

Distributed by:
Itasca Books
5120 Cedar Lake Road
Minneapolis, MN 55416
Phones: 952-345-4488/1-800-901-3480
Fax: 952-920-0541

Copies of this book can be ordered at:
www.seriousaboutretiring.com

TO

Lucy Rose
and
Jay and Dilek

CONTENTS

PART THREE
Making It Work

SERIOUS
ABOUT
RETIRING

Preface

Some fathers and sons go fishing or hunting or go to ballgames together. My father and I spent a lot of time—on Saturday morning walks starting when I was eight years old—talking about stocks, which was his hobby; they became my hobby too. Growing up, I read every book in our small-town upper New York State public library about investing.

Before entering high school, I used money I had saved to buy stock in Fargo Oil (a Canadian company) and in a mutual fund, Axe Science and Electronics. In high school, I tracked price and volume movements of stocks via graphs, bought and sold short, and purchased options and futures.

Entering Brandeis University in 1961, I majored in chemistry. Sputnik was in the news, and science was hailed as the path to the future. In 1969, I earned a PhD in chemistry from UC Berkeley, then did a postdoctoral fellowship at the University of Wisconsin, Madison, and taught biochemistry at the University of Massachusetts, Amherst.

My wife and I moved to the Twin Cities when she, newly armed with a PhD, took a teaching position at the University of Minnesota,

Minneapolis. I decided to use my computer background from my graduate studies and worked in the emerging field of business computers. I took night classes at the university to earn an MBA. All this time, I saved money and invested it; this was still my hobby and I schooled myself further about investments and finance. Friends and colleagues began coming to me for investment advice.

In 1985 I was laid off from my job in computers. One evening soon afterward, my wife got together with some friends to discuss what I might do next. They concluded that my love of investing made it natural for me to become a stockbroker. At first, I thought that was a ridiculous idea, because I had never been a salesperson. After a few days I concluded that it was worth exploring. I didn't become a stockbroker. Instead, in my forties I began a new career as a Certified Financial Planner (CFP) in the life insurance/investment field.

My background in research, analysis, and teaching proved to be relevant and invaluable. I analyzed clients' situations, helped them manage their investments, kept up with the financial research literature, and taught classes.

After doing financial planning for twenty-nine years, working with hundreds of families in a range of financial and personal circumstances, I decided to semi-retire—continue working with a small number of clients and do other things. For example, I began bicycling more seriously and took up the cello.

I wanted to use my experience in financial planning to give something back. So, in 2015 I began writing this book, condensing insights gained over the years. I hope it will help you make a smooth and fulfilling transition to that next major chapter of your life.

WHO IS THIS BOOK FOR?

Are you getting serious about retiring? If you are anywhere from ten years before to five years after departure from the workforce—that's you. This is when you identify issues and consider your options. It is the time to make key decisions as you start your new life. This book will help you with those decisions.

Most likely, you fall into one of these categories:

1. *You are not sure what you want to do when you retire.* Perhaps you have been particularly successful in your career. If so, you have derived not just income but also the fulfillment that comes from using your skills, energy, and creativity on a daily basis. Why would you ever want to do anything else? Why would you want to go from a hundred miles an hour to zero overnight? And yet, you may have a sense that there could be something more and better in retirement. If so, this book will offer you many ideas about what you might do and how you can proceed.

2. *You know what you want to do, but you are not sure how to get there.* This book contains many practical ideas for making progress in a wide range of areas.

3. *You have a very clear idea of what you want to do and how to do it.* Even so, this book will have some twists and turns you might not have anticipated.

HOW CAN YOU USE THIS BOOK?

Here are two main challenges in making good decisions for retirement. One is that you don't know what you don't know. The concepts in this book will alert you to issues you might not have considered before.

The other challenge involves the uncertainties you may face. For example, will you have serious health, financial, or emotional problems? Will you have the resources to transcend whatever issues you encounter?

This book addresses what you can do with your time, how you can help maintain good health, how much money you will need to have the life you want, the kinds of returns you will get on your investments, how to identify where your retirement income will come from, and how long you will need your stream of income in the future.

There is no single best path for the process of retiring. Your particular circumstances and values affect your decisions and path. As well, your skills, resources, and personal traits are important in how your retirement unfolds. But each chapter in this book advises on the next steps to take as you prepare to retire.

What is your approach to life? Are you more of an opportunist or a planner? The opportunist's style includes little planning and forethought, capitalizing on opportunities as they arise, going with the flow. The planner's style, on the other hand, involves arranging all details in advance. Both styles can work; most people use a mixture of the two.

If you are an opportunist, you can use this book to identify possible options to take advantage of. If you are more intentional, this book can help in your planning. For either style, it will help you to collect ideas about how to proceed, prioritize them, and set them in motion.

This book differs in several important ways from other books on retirement:

- Its focus is on retiring, not on retirement—hence the book's title. Each substantive chapter contains a section on the first steps to take in preparing for the transition to retirement.
- The approach to the topics addressed is holistic and comprehensive. Various topics are interrelated and should not be seen in isolation. For example, travel, housing, relationships, and income all affect one another.
- Retiring is an individual journey, not a destination. Exploring your many alternatives, you will come to understand better what is really important for you, individually. Since you might change your philosophy and activities over time, some ideas in this book that are not relevant now could become helpful later.
- The ideas presented here are based on my own semiretirement as well as on the experiences of hundreds of families I have met and helped over the past thirty years.

- Interwoven through the book are case studies based on experiences of the fictional extended Miller family that are composites of various people I have helped during my career; they are introduced beginning on page xix. These individuals are of different ages and in different circumstances; this is to illustrate how people dealing with the same general issues can come to different conclusions about what they want and need to do.

Here is an overview.

Part One
What Gets You Up in the Morning:
Connections, Explorations, Contributions
The time of retirement comes with many opportunities. Some activities will excite and nourish you, antidotes to filling the time with routine activities and having nothing to show for it.

1. More Hours, More Years
In retirement, you will not only have more time each day but also more years left than you might think. You will also have more opportunities to take advantage of, particularly if you can overcome any challenges presented by money, health, and personal relationships.

2. So Many Choices, So Little Time
What does it mean to feel truly alive in retirement? How do you lead a life during that time that is singularly meaningful to you?

3. Think Big
What would you do differently if you believed you would have enough time to accomplish something truly great in retirement?

4. Going Everywhere and Seeing Everything
Since you will have more time and flexibility available in retirement, you might want to see the world. You can travel to a wide range of places by yourself or with groups.

5. Your Housing and Your Life

You will have many possibilities for how and where to live in retirement. Maybe you will stay put, or maybe not. A change could help you achieve a more desired lifestyle. How does money affect housing possibilities and choice of locations?

6. Love and Support

Leaving a work environment means leaving behind your job-based social networks. How can family and friends augment the quality of your relationships in retirement?

7. Blood and Money

In retirement, family and money are intertwined. What roles will money play in relationships with family members?

8. The Hereafter

Since you cannot take your money with you when you die, you will need estate planning. What legal documents will facilitate ownership transfers on death? What role might charitable planning have in these transfers?

9. If You Don't Have Your Health . . .

Chronic health problems in retirement can differ from those in preretirement. What tactics can you use to manage your health and energy successfully?

10. Coming up with Money for Healthcare

There are two health insurance systems that provide healthcare when you need it: Medicare, its supplements, and alternatives; and long-term-care insurance. What resources can you use to pay for your healthcare?

Part Two

What Lets You Sleep at Night: Enough Money

Aside from health, the most common concern of retirees and pre-retirees is about having enough money for the life they want. This part of the book provides background on how investments work and how to include them in plans for a successful retirement.

11. Enough Money for What?
Your two most important tools for determining how much will be enough are budgeting and projections. How can you use those tools?

12. Expenses = Lifestyle
What alternatives do you have for cutting and managing expenses, especially if there is a gap between actual and desired lifestyles?

13. Investment Income
What strategies can you use to provide safe and sustainable investment income during retirement? What does the latest financial research say?

14. Income from Other Sources
What sources of retirement income will you have besides investments? How do work-oriented benefits, part-time work, and Social Security as well as loans, gifts, or other types of compensation from friends and relatives fit in?

15. The Right Investment Ingredients
You can choose from a huge range of investments types, both traditional and those previously available only to the wealthy. You can purchase investments individually or as pooled assets. How can you evaluate and select high-quality investments?

16. The Right Investment Mix
How can you diversify investments to build a sturdy investment portfolio?

17. Taxes: The Tail That Wags the Dog
The proper use of tax-advantaged buckets, such as IRAs, Roth IRAs, and personal accounts, will have a huge effect on your taxes in retirement. Which investments go where, and how should you take cash out of the different buckets?

18. Planning Anyhow

What role does planning play in preparing for retirement? What are the two necessary plans that must be completed?

Part Three

Making It Work

Because of the complexity of choices involved, you might get stuck putting it all together. This section discusses ways you can make needed progress in managing the process of retiring.

19. Getting Help

What can you do when you do not know what you do not know? How do you choose friends, relatives and professional advisors to get help? How do professional advisors work and what do they charge?

20. Your Best Years Yet

What ideas and strategies can you use to organize your time in retirement so that these years are fun and meaningful?

Introducing the Millers

Members of the Miller family, whose stories are woven throughout the book, are fictitious. They are, however, composites of real people. I use case studies involving them to illustrate situations you might recognize.

The Millers who are the focus of the case studies are of varying ages and in various situations. They include the matriarch, Sue, and her four adult children—Annie, Becky, Cathy, and Doug—and their spouses. For each of them, retirement likely, but not necessarily, means giving up jobs and paychecks. They will need to resolve matters related to income, lifestyle, and expenses in different ways. Not working frees up time for other things. And they no longer have to live near their workplaces, so they might be free to move.

The process of retiring has its own challenges for each of them and their spouses:

- They will face decisions, such as when to retire and how to shape their futures.
- They will need to make those decisions in spite of the unknowns, including what their health and financial conditions might be.

- They do not know what they do not know. Even knowing the right questions to ask is a challenge.
- They will find too much advice available to them, often contradictory, when facing their decisions. They will probably want some reliable help in the process.

Each of the Miller siblings and their spouses has questions about what to do and when. It is critical for them to have enough money to last them the rest of their lives.

They will have many "how" questions: How do they set up their investments? How do they draw an income from them? How do family, health, housing, and taxes affect their plans? Their most immediate question, though, is how to navigate the process of retiring.

SUE, THE MATRIARCH

Sue met her husband, Keith, just after World War II. Right after graduating from high school, they had both found jobs at the Factory and met there. They dated, married, and had three girls and a boy.

Eighteen years into their marriage, Keith died of a massive heart attack. Besides Sue, he left behind daughters Annie (sixteen), Becky (ten), and Cathy (four) and son Doug (two). Sue never remarried. She and her children have always been close. Sue went back to work at The Factory and stayed for twenty-five years, supporting herself and her children. Then she retired.

Now ninety years old and widowed for more than fifty years, Sue is still chugging away on her own. She lives independently and drives occasionally, though her children have been encouraging her to hand over the car keys. She loves to quilt and spend time with her flock of grandchildren and, now, her great-grandchildren. Her daughters Annie and Cathy live out of town in a city not too far away. Her daughter Becky and son, Doug, live close by and help Mom occasionally, as needed.

ANNIE, THE OLDEST

Annie, seventy years old and re-cently widowed, is thinking about retiring. She loves her work as an at-torney for nonprofits—helping the poor with housing issues. She also serves on the boards of a few non-profits. Annie is a doer, known for her passion for making the world a better place.

In high school, Annie couldn't wait to leave town and go to college. As a student at Berkeley in the 1960s, she protested America's in-volvement in the Vietnam War, and she has remained an activist to this day. She met her future husband, Al, ironically a Vietnam vet-eran, at a political rally after finishing law school. He was tall, hand-some, and six years older than Annie. Al became an activist attorney. The two lived together for a few years, married, and set up a law prac-tice together.

The couple were unable to have children, and did not adopt any. Annie was looking forward to celebrating fifty years of marriage. But three months ago, Al, who had long been a heavy smoker, died of lung cancer. Annie had taken an extended leave from work in order to care for him in his last months.

Still in mourning, she is uncertain about how to proceed. She won-ders what her life would be like if she decided to retire soon.

BECKY, THE MIDDLE DAUGHTER, AND HER HUSBAND, BRIAN

Becky, sixty-four, is thinking about the upcoming party marking her retirement from the elementary school where she has taught for forty years. This is the same school she attended as a child, and the one to which she returned to teach after college. She has been there long enough to have among her pupils the grandchildren of her first students.

Becky worked her way through teachers college with the help of a scholarship. She moved back to town in part to support Sue and her younger siblings, Cathy and Doug. Working at the elementary school, she met another young teacher, Phil. They married a year later and had a child but then divorced. But Phil remained a close friend, so they were able to raise their child jointly.

Attending her fifteen-year high school reunion as a divorcée, Becky reconnected with Brian, her high school sweetheart. His wife had died a few years earlier of breast cancer, and now he was raising his two kids on his own. Brian and Becky quickly fell in love, married, and had a child. They have now been wed for thirty years. Besides their four offspring, they also have six wonderful grandchildren.

Until recently, neither of them thought much about retiring. They are both healthy and have been focused on work and family. But now Becky will be leaving the school. And Brian, sixty-five, who was just laid off from the sales job he has held for seventeen years, is debating whether to go back to work or retire.

CATHY, THE YOUNGEST DAUGHTER, AND HER HUSBAND, CHUCK

At fifty-eight, Cathy is starting to do some retirement-related calculations and planning. She is the Miller daughter who has always been good with numbers. After college, she did tax work in an accounting firm for a few years.

Then she met Chuck (now sixty-one), who managed his family's restaurant, The Captain's Table. (Captain was the nickname of his father, Bill, who had held that rank in the Navy during World War II.) Cathy and Chuck married, and she pitched right into the business, acting as a needed mediating and stabilizing influence. Chuck and Cathy have been running The Captain's Table jointly for a few decades. (Bill is still a part owner but quit daily operations some years ago following a series of health problems.) The couple split the work responsibilities: he does the day-to-day management, while she handles the financials. Their business has marched forward in a pretty much straight line. In fact, Cathy just negotiated the opening of two new Captain's Tables in town.

Courtney, the oldest of Chuck and Cathy's three children, works in the business and is assuming increased responsibility. Indeed, she may soon be ready to run one of the new restaurants. Chuck's sister, his only sibling, is not part of the business but is an active member of the family.

Chuck and Cathy are starting to think about what to do next. Maybe they do not have to work quite so hard.

Maybe there is a life outside of running The Captain's Table. The idea of spending more time hunting and fishing appeals to Chuck. And Cathy would like to spend more time with her grandchildren.

DOUG, THE YOUNGEST OF THE FOUR MILLER SIBLINGS

Doug, fifty-six, is a cellist. He just landed a very good gig as a long-term substitute player in the local symphony orchestra. He knows its musicians well and has played with them many times, but not as often as he would like. He is a good enough musician that he can be called in at the last minute to step in for someone else.

As a young child, Doug loved to sing and play piano. His first music teacher, who understood the Millers' financial situation and saw Doug's enthusiasm, let him take some lessons pro bono. When he was nine, he became quite interested in the cello, switched to it, and has been playing it all these years.

He majored in music at the local college and has been a working musician ever since. But the work has been spotty. Through the years, he has supported himself by waiting tables at a restaurant, cleaning hotel rooms, and parking cars, among other such jobs.

Everyone loves Doug, particularly his older sisters, who treated him like their pet when he was young. Even though he now leads a life that many people would consider to be financially challenging, he is always upbeat and passionate about music.

Doug has heard his older sisters starting to talk about retirement. He has almost no savings and no partner to help support him. He is beginning to wonder what he needs to do next.

• • •

I have noted general facts about members of the extended Miller family to suggest how they might view the prospect of retirement. You may see some similarities between their situations and your own. But yours, naturally, will be subject to the particulars of your health, family relationships, fiscal resources, values, and interests, which together will help shape your approach to retirement.

THE MILLER FAMILY TREE

{Name} = Deceased

Sue, 90 — {Keith}

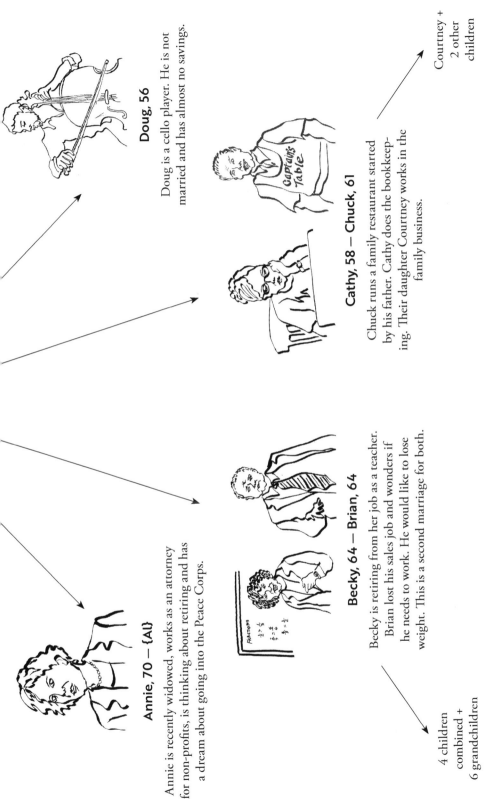

Doug, 56

Doug is a cello player. He is not married and has almost no savings.

Cathy, 58 — Chuck, 61

Chuck runs a family restaurant started by his father. Cathy does the bookkeeping. Their daughter Courtney works in the family business.

Courtney + 2 other children

Annie, 70 — {Al}

Annie is recently widowed, works as an attorney for non-profits, is thinking about retiring and has a dream about going into the Peace Corps.

Becky, 64 — Brian, 64

Becky is retiring from her job as a teacher. Brian lost his sales job and wonders if he needs to work. He would like to lose weight. This is a second marriage for both.

4 children combined + 6 grandchildren

PART ONE

What Gets You Up in the Morning: Connections, Explorations, Contributions

For some people, not knowing what they will do in retirement is a serious issue that can even keep them postponing when they retire. Others cannot wait to retire. They are excited about the opportunities to do what they really want to do.

The purpose of this section is to call your attention to the many possibilities that you have to connect and explore. This potential is coupled with the challenges of aging itself, particularly health and mortality issues. As in other parts of life, you will have surprises, some good and some not so good. The success of your retirement will depend not just on what happens to you but also on how you handle decisions and adapt.

1. More Hours, More Years

As you look forward to retirement, are you thinking that you have worked hard for years and soon will be able to relax? Do you think of retirement as time for yourself? Do you think that goals are for working people, not retirees? Are you contemplating a slower pace that will include time to do nothing? You might end up having much more time in retirement than you imagine. You may well have more hours per day and more years ahead than you think.

During the working years, your largest concentration of free time is generally on weekends. A lot of daily nonwork time is taken up with eating, sleeping, and domestic obligations. Some of those obligations often spill over into the weekend.

By adding up your present per-week working and commuting hours, you will, in theory anyway, see how much additional free time you will have each week in retirement. In one year of retirement, you can potentially have as much free time as you have had in the previous five to twenty working years combined.

Now, think how many years of free time you might have when retired. Perhaps you are familiar with current U.S. life-expectancy numbers: seventy-six for men and eighty-one for women. These are the numbers for newborns and so not particularly relevant for you. Here are several more appropriate such numbers to consider, based on your current age:

LIFE EXPECTANCY BY AGE

Age	Men	Women
60	81	84
70	84	86
80	88	90
90	94	95

Remember what life expectancy means. If you are a member of a group of one hundred thousand sixty-year-old women of average health and genetics, you can expect that by the time you are eighty-four, half of your group will have died and fifty thousand will still be alive. That means you will have a fifty-fifty chance of lasting beyond your current life expectancy—perhaps well beyond it.

Perhaps you estimate your prospects based on how long your parents or other relatives lived. But are you taking advances in medicine into account? Life expectancies have been increasing approximately two years per decade for the last century or more. Say, for example, that your parents were born thirty years before you and each died at age seventy-five. Taking those factors into account, today you would die at eighty-one.

Medical research marches on, with advances in diagnosis and treatment emerging all the time. Unless the United States suffers an uncontrolled plague or a war, life expectancies will probably continue increasing markedly during your lifetime.

TIME FEELS DIFFERENT AS YOU AGE

No matter what choices you make, time passes quickly. On a day-to-day basis, your activities will fill your time like air rushing into a vacuum. You will probably feel busy no matter what you do. Many retirees say they do not understand how they had the time to work before they retired.

As well, the months and years seem to slip by more quickly. Your number of years to live, especially good years, is unpredictable. In any case, unless you get very sick, you probably will not know how much time you have left.

Because of the potential for many years of free time, you may want to consider a "Think Small/Think Big" approach.

"Think Small" means planning what you want to do if you learn your time is relatively short. Which activities do you want to pursue? What places do you want to go? If you have a bucket list, this is the time to look at it and determine your highest priorities. Then do those things soon, while you still can.

"Think Big" means planning what you want to do if your time is long. You may live to ninety-five or even a hundred, which is becoming less unusual. What is your dream? If your time is long, you could have enough of it to further hone a skill you already have or even cultivate a new one. You could learn a language or a take up a musical instrument. You could develop an expertise or a hobby. You could launch a major project that contributes to your family or your community. If you pick an area that excites you, the worst that can happen is that you do not see the project all the way through. But you would probably have had a great time along the way.

ANNIE AND AUNT DELORES

As Annie ponders what she might want to do in widowhood, she thinks a lot about her favorite aunt, Delores, her mother's older sister. Now ninety-five, Delores has outlived three husbands, has had a variety of careers, and is still going strong. She has been an inspiration for Annie.

For the past decade, Annie has been wondering how many years she might have left to work, travel, volunteer, and do whatever else she wants to do. Of course, she cannot know how long she will live.

She will have some control over that, to the extent that she engages in healthy behaviors. Her real questions should be about what to do with however much time she has.

If she assumes she will live as long as Aunt Delores—another twenty-five years—even that might prove to be an underestimate, because Delores may have several good years left herself. And since life expectancy has been increasing by two years per decade, Annie could live to a hundred, or beyond. With those things in mind, she begins focusing on what she might do and accomplish.

THE CHALLENGES OF HAVING ALL THAT TIME

An abundance of time presents major challenges in the domains of money, health, and relationships.

The first challenge concerns the fact that you want your money to last longer than you do. If you end up having a lot of time, which is quite possible, you will need to have more money than if you die within a relatively few years. If you have a partner, things are a little more complicated, that is, your money needs to last over both of your lifetimes. A joint lifetime is the age at which the last member of a couple dies. It is approximately seven years longer than your individual lifetimes. So the money may have to last even longer than you may estimate.

Lifetime-benefit programs can help ensure that your money lasts as long as you do. Social Security and defined-benefit pensions from work keep paying as long as you live. There are also annuity products with lifetime guarantees that can be helpful.

If you do not have investments that include guarantees, you should organize your portfolio with an eye to weathering any future economic storms. If you live a long time, the odds are that you will experience some serious economic events.

Inflation compounds the problem. To maintain your standard of living throughout your lifetime, your income needs to increase from year to year. If inflation is at a 3.5 percent rate, costs will nearly triple over a thirty-year time frame.

The second challenge lies in the area of health. You may develop chronic disabilities that need to be managed. Over time, your organs, tissues, and one or more of your physiological systems may break down.

In terms of health problems, the key thing is not to let them overwhelm everything in your retirement life. You can have at least some control here by minimizing bad habits and maintaining weight and energy through proper nutrition and exercise. After all, you want to be *alive*, and not just technically.

The third challenge has to do with your relationships. Your mental health depends in part on having vital and intimate social contacts. As you age, you are likely to lose people you love, both family and friends. Though loved ones are irreplaceable, you still need to maintain ties with people you care about and who care about you. So, you need to be part of a community—this could be a residential community or a faith community—or even several communities.

PREPARING FOR ALL THAT TIME IN RETIREMENT

Your first step is to acknowledge and embrace the idea that your retirement might be a long one. Then, think about your concerns and hopes for the coming years. What are your dreams? What holds you back? Writing down the answers to these questions could help you develop more clarity about the potentials of retirement.

The challenges will emerge by themselves. The opportunities you might take advantage of will require your direct involvement.

It is constructive to start Thinking Small and Thinking Big before you retire. Here is the chance to let your imagination and creativity bring you to new places, literally and figuratively.

2. So Many Choices, So Little Time

For some people, the transition to retirement comes as quite a shock. Typically, Americans are overworked and under-vacationed when compared to people in other developed countries. Some cannot wait to retire. Others dread the prospect: what are they going to do with all that time if they are not working?

If you are like most people, however, you do have some idea of what you want to do. You have two to-do lists, the first one comprised of things you want and need to do within the short-to-intermediate future. The second is a bucket list, containing things you ideally want to do but are not sure you will be able to do.

Here are some items commonly found on such lists:

- spending time with other people, including grandchildren, other relatives, and friends
- working part-time, either paid or unpaid volunteering
- recreational activities, including hobbies, regular physical exercise, pursuing sports such as fishing and golf, reading, communicating via the Internet, and going to concerts
- domestic activities, including work on the house or garden

- travel
- creative expression through arts and crafts, such as writing, painting, and the performing arts—instrumental and vocal music, dance, and theater

Some see retirement as a destination; others see it as a path. If you are in the second group, you realize that retirement can be a time of discovery and change.

BRIAN AND HIS SUDDEN JOB LOSS

Brian is upset about being unexpectedly laid off from his sales job after having worked hard at it for seventeen years. He was not ready for this, but like other people who lose their jobs or have a health problem that prevents them from working, he will have to make decisions anyway. At the moment, he is unsure whether he wants to, or needs to, find another position.

Abrupt job loss can be emotionally challenging. Brian has lost not just his job and income but also his routine associations with colleagues and clients, the structure of work time, and the rewards of accomplishing things.

Confusing the situation is that he does not know what he would do if he were to retire now. Brian knows that he needs to be around people—that was the part of his job he most enjoyed. He regrets not having built something on his own, such as a business. Another thing he knows is that he is much too heavy and needs to do something about it. He was in the habit of taking clients out to lunch, and the weight gradually accumulated. If he had more time, he thinks, he would find a way to take off that extra weight.

Brian will have to figure out if he needs to find work or if he and Becky will have enough income if he doesn't. If he does have to work, he will start networking with friends and colleagues to find out his alternatives and opportunities. If he does not need the income, he may still want to find an appealing part-time job; this would also involve networking.

Brian can take one of two approaches to retirement. He may want to jump into the water and start a variety of activities. Or he might like to wade in gradually. He is most likely to succeed if he includes the activities in his life that he feels most passionate about. Researching and planning for them could be a high priority for him.

When Brian makes his to-do list, he will identify some "shoulds," such as his desire to lose weight. If it starts to look as if those activities are not going to happen, then one approach would be for him to begin an activity involving others. It could be a class or exercising with friends. Whatever he can do to build in accountability will help him accomplish what he "should" do.

Brian's life will be enjoyable if he maintains a positive attitude about the time suddenly opening up before him. This could be a chance for him to explore a wider range of work, volunteer, and leisure opportunities than he has thought about before. He can think of this moment as a sabbatical from work, an exploration and renewal. He can even try traveling or cultivate a hobby.

If Brian feels distressed and confused about losing his job, a support group might be helpful. He could share stories with others and realize that he is not alone. Such a group would help him emotionally and might give him practical clues about how to proceed.

BEING TRULY ALIVE

Here is an interesting way to think about the mix of activities you want to cultivate during your retirement. Are there some necessary activities that, if you do not include them in the mix, could have serious long-term consequences on the quality of your retirement? It turns out there has been research addressing this question based on interviews with retirees to learn what has worked and not worked for them.

Gerontologist Lucy Rose Fischer and several colleagues have developed a model, called ALIVE, to summarize research in this area. The ALIVE acronym stands for Activity, Learning, Intimacy, Vitality, and Engagement. These five elements of well-being all work together for those who reach their peak.

Activity means physical activity. A wide range of research has shown that exercise can improve the quality of your life on several levels. Along with good nutrition, it can help postpone physical deterioration and help provide the energy needed for an active life. Regular exercise enables you to lessen stress and recharge.

Learning means using your mind through such activities as reading, listening, brainstorming, and puzzle-solving, helping to ensure cognitive well-being. Such mental activity is analogous to physical activity. Gerontologist Gene Cohen calls it "sweating with the mind." Learning can help forestall mental deterioration and facilitate everyday problem-solving.

Intimacy means having close relationships with people you know well. Intimacy is important for emotional well-being, preventing social isolation, and potentially increasing both longevity and quality of life. At its best, intimacy provides support and encouragement. A friend or family member can help you do what you say that you want to do—and can provide hope.

Vitality comes from having a positive attitude. Vitality is infectious; it helps if you surround yourself with people who embody that trait. For some, spirituality is a component of vitality; this may be connected to active participation in a faith community.

Engagement means taking part in the life of a larger society. Social interactions contribute to well-being. You can be socially engaged by volunteering or participating in various types of community organizations or groups.

CHALLENGES TO GETTING THIS RIGHT: WHAT YOU ACTUALLY DO IN RETIREMENT

Your life will not be as structured in retirement as it was when you were working. Given that, it can be easy to drift and let inertia take over. But an intentional approach—planning and doing things purposefully—can have huge benefits.

Of course, you may be limited in what you can do by your available resources—money, income, energy, and health. This is where creativity and imagination come into play—the old "where there is a will, there is a way" approach. But the "will" comes first. Do you have any outcomes in mind? If so, what do you need to do to make them happen?

PREPARING FOR WHAT YOU WANT TO DO

Here is an assignment to help you begin creating a deeper, more meaningful retirement.

Start with the list of what you want to do, plus your bucket list, as described above. Your goal should be to expand the original list as much as possible before you start to rule things out. Brainstorming, in other words. Here are some questions to ask yourself that might refine your list.

- What achievements are you proudest of? Can you pursue similar activities that will also provide satisfaction?
- What needs to happen over the first three years of retirement for you to feel your time has been well spent? Where will you be, and what will you do?
- Which activities would you like to expand upon in retirement, and which ones would you like to whittle down?
- If you had more time and money than you needed, what would you do differently?

- Do you have any regrets? If so, what can you do to address them now?
- What are you good at, a talent or skill you might even take for granted? What activities give you energy?

These questions are rich and worth spending some time on. It helps to write your answers down. You can share them with others to get feedback and perhaps improve them. Consider involving people whom you know well from a variety of contexts—life partners, family members, longtime friends, and work colleagues. You might be surprised at the variety of responses you receive.

Some of the ideas you will generate concern activities or projects you (or others) feel you "should" do. Maybe you will do them because they must be done. But the activities that get you up in the morning are those that are exciting enough that you cannot wait to get going.

Even if all your ideas are wonderful, you do not have to act on them all, and certainly not at once. You will find that retirement is a process, not a fixed state of being. Your activities will morph as you gather new information.

3. Think Big

The large block of time you may have in retirement enables you to think big. Almost any activity you choose to do can be expanded upon. Here are some examples:

- *Reading.* If you read fiction, you might go to the places depicted. You could write a book, articles, stories, or essays. You could take writing courses to help kick-start that process.

  If you read nonfiction, this could be the start of delving into whole new subjects. You could take courses and accumulate enough information and skills to be involved in whole new learning ventures.

- *The arts.* If, for example, you are passionate about listening to music, why not learn an instrument? It might take years to gain some mastery or to play the kind of music you like best, but so what? If it turns out that you do not have the time or health to go all the way, you will still have enjoyed the learning process.

- *Sports.* Of course, you can watch them on television or via the Internet or go to live games. Or you can play in a league if it is a team sport or coach others. Or you can support teams financially and promote them in various ways.

- *Food.* This could be the focus of a hobby in retirement, either learning more about cooking or perhaps volunteering at food banks or helping prepare meals for homeless people.

Thinking big will add color to your life, give you a sense of purpose, and thereby make your life more meaningful and joyful. When older people are asked what they most regret, they often say they wish they had taken more risks. They wish they had tried more activities, even if some of them might have failed. With retirement in front of you, there may be many more wonderful possibilities than you think.

CHUCK'S BIG IDEA

Chuck is sixty-one and feeling restless. With the help of Cathy and, now, his daughter Courtney, he is about to open two new Captain's Table restaurants. But he would like to expand his activities in other directions as well.

Chuck is recognized by his peers as a successful business owner. Years ago, he attended a regional meeting of the National Restaurant Association. He came to the meeting with a good reputation and known leadership qualities, and drew attention for his active participation in discussions. As a result, he was encouraged to join the association's board of directors. But he decided not to pursue it, being too busy at work.

Now Chuck wonders if he should consider getting involved in the association. It could provide him with a great opportunity to meet other successful business owners. Some of them likewise might be building family-based restaurant chains, so he could pick their brains. Also, some might be thinking about transitioning out of their businesses and dealing with ownership succession.

Chuck has long been interested in all aspects of food. Lately, he has become keenly interested in the pervasive problem of hunger. It seems crazy to him. With all the food around, how could there possibly be so many hungry people? What have other communities done about this stubborn challenge? What ideas can he offer to fight hunger in his community?

You can extrapolate some aspects of Chuck's situation into your own:

- Chuck may now be in the most productive time of his life. If he wants, he can make large contributions in a variety of areas as he gets older.
- In order to make his urge to help fight hunger amount to something, he will need to commit to making something happen.
- Chuck has numerous qualities to offer: leadership and interpersonal skills, good work habits, an understanding of what it takes to be a successful restaurateur, and a solid reputation. He also has the support of a great staff, including his wife and daughter.
- Being an active member of the National Restaurant Association could be a huge asset in working on the problem of hunger. The association may already have programs in his area. He might be able to recruit fellow association members to work with him. He could forge strategic relationships between the association and other groups nationwide committed to dealing with this social ill.
- It may not matter to Chuck if he gets paid to do such work. So, if he did, how would you classify it: work or retirement?
- Moving into retirement does not have to be an all-or-nothing proposition—one day you are working, the next retired. It can be gradual. In fact, if Chuck becomes immersed in helping combat hunger, he might delegate more of his responsibilities to his daughter, and continue with the parts of his business he enjoys most.

The notion of phased retirement has become increasingly common at firms and organizations of all sizes. This can involve cutting back on job hours over a period of a few years' while increasing the amount of time spent on other activities.

A NEW BEGINNING

Retirement has some elements in common with the time when you first entered the workforce. Both periods offer opportunities to reset your life and choose activities for the next stage of life. But there are important differences as well.

Here are the challenges: Maybe you have less energy than when you were younger. And the chronological scope has changed, because now your remaining time seems more finite than it did when you were younger.

But there are advantages. Unlike the time when you began working, you might need to earn less money now. You may have enough money saved to provide at least partial support. You probably can make mistakes in your retirement pursuits without putting your career at risk. Also, the relatively limited amount of time allotted to you can be a stimulant to making personal progress.

OVERCOMING YOUR LIMITATIONS

Does a retirement span of ten to thirty years rule out most possibilities? Not necessarily. Many working situations today entail assembling teams with the right skills in order to accomplish set objectives within time frames ranging from a few weeks to a few years. So, your ten to thirty years of retirement could give you chances to work on multiple projects.

When making your list of things to do in retirement, did you automatically eliminate those requiring more money or time than you believe you have? Can your money enable you to do "cool" things, or does everything you are passionate about seem out of reach?

You can draw upon whatever resources you have when starting to think and act big:

- You have substantial self-knowledge. You know what you like and what you don't like. You are aware of your strengths and weaknesses.
- You have a fund of employment experience that provides information, skills, and deep knowledge. For example, you may have learned a lot about at least one industry—its challenges and opportunities. Other jobs may have taught you about applying technology in a variety of circumstances. Perhaps you have been exposed to marketing or research or finance or production techniques. Or you may have served in a managerial/leadership role.
- You may have been to college. Perhaps you took courses in the humanities, social sciences, the arts, science, and math. Are there topics from these courses that appeal to you now?
- Your aptitudes can be a major resource. These can include facility with numbers, text analysis, or the arts. You may also possess communication skills, such as an ability to simplify complicated concepts or to structure win-win situations.
- Various community resources are available, including libraries, social-support agencies, and nonprofits.
- Friends and family can supply you with support, ideas, their own experience, and contacts that can help expand your personal network. Interactions with others can also enable you to undertake activities that you might prefer not to—or even be able to—pursue on your own.

VOLUNTEERING AS A BIG ACTIVITY

The traditional kind of volunteering involves working with a nonprofit that provides a community service of some kind. Depending on the scope of your involvement, volunteering can be a big activity during retirement.

Typically, volunteering increases as you age, because retirees have more time for it. Any financial contributions that you make to the nonprofit, either while you are alive or upon death, are a way to augment your involvement.

For some people, volunteering comes naturally. It is just a way of giving back. For others, volunteering feels more like something they *should* do. In fact, many retirees never get around to volunteering at all.

There is an entirely different way of thinking about volunteering via nonprofit organizations, which is that it is a way of doing a bit to change the world in ways that are important for you. In this view, a nonprofit becomes a partner to help you achieve what you want. It starts with a vision of how you would like the world or your community to be different and better.

Here is an example: Perhaps you are aware that children who do not learn to read at an early age could be permanently disadvantaged with respect to finding decent employment as adults. So, it might be valuable to tutor a child at a school or library.

And another example. You watch a TV news report about the plight of people ravaged by a terrible storm, and you want to help. You could do something on your own, perhaps make a financial contribution.

If that is not enough and you want to think bigger, you could identify a nonprofit whose mission is to help people caught in such weather events and volunteer for it. Such organizations help you use your time, money, and skills to accomplish more than you could on your own. Working with a nonprofit, you can think about the knowledge you might bring to bear that would help them be more effective.

Volunteering has its own forms of nonmonetary compensation, including the satisfaction of being involved, a sense of belonging to a community, recognition for your efforts, and appreciation from the people being helped.

If you don't know which volunteering experience might be right for you, there are nonprofits, such as RSVP, that are set up to help match your interests, skills, and experience to an organization and volunteer experience.

There is another important kind of volunteering: helping family members, friends, and neighbors by devoting time or money to them. You might help care for your grandchildren or for parents who need your attention.

For many retirees, a combination of helping both family and community can be fulfilling.

WORKING AS A BIG ACTIVITY

Perhaps you cannot afford to volunteer because you need a part-time job and the income it provides. Can you see being employed as a means of doing something you really want to do? This might translate to finding work at an organization or helping start a new business, nonprofit, or for-profit whose mission you can embrace. You can have a part-time job and still engage in various other "retirement" activities.

And if you hate the part-time work, what then? If a major motivation for retiring is getting to do what you really want to do, then perhaps retiring may be less about your age than about your sense of purpose. The main things to consider are how and where to use your resources.

PREPARING FOR A BIG RETIREMENT

Thinking big always starts with assessing your passions and then acting on them. You can start working on an idea at home. Or you can combine your efforts with those of others.

If you have already generated a list of possibilities for what you want to do (see Chapter 2), then now is the time to decide which of them, either singly or in combination, have the potential to make your life bigger. Putting the list on paper will facilitate talking possibilities over with others—extremely helpful in your development of new ideas.

Choosing and starting a big activity will probably involve some research on your part—where, when, how. There is no reason you cannot start thinking and planning while you are winding down your preretirement working life. Are you getting excited about your future?

4. Going Everywhere and Seeing Everything

Many people start traveling early in retirement. Indeed, more and better travel is among the most common aspirations of people who are serious about retiring.

Travel can be an adventure, a time that provides warm memories, and an occasion to visit or explore special places—learning and experiencing new things along the way.

There are several reasons why travel can be a focus in early retirement:

1. You may have more energy and better health now than you will later on.
2. You may have trips in mind that you have not had enough time to take while working with a limited allowance of vacation days.
3. You may have accumulated more money over the past few decades, some of which you can now spend travelling.

There is almost no limit to where you can go. The travel industry will help you get to where you want to go, find food and housing, and guide you to sights and sites. There are simplified packages available—just sign up, pay the money, and show up. The most complete ones include destination parks such as Disneyland, resorts, guided tours, and cruises on which you can visit multiple places without having to repack your suitcases. Or you can take a trip that simply involves driving to a cabin and hanging out.

Perhaps you are looking for the perfect place to visit, or there is a place on your bucket list that you feel you must see. Searching for, finding, and then experiencing the perfect trip is an accomplishment to talk about with family and friends.

ANNIE THINKS ABOUT ACTING ON A LONG-AGO DREAM—THE PEACE CORPS

Annie never joined the Peace Corps, but she and her late husband Al thought a lot about it through the years. Annie may have the time now for an adventure like this. She knows that homelessness, which is her professional interest and her passion, is not the same in all countries, and she wonders what she could learn elsewhere to bring back to her efforts in the United States. Being in the Peace Corps would be a wonderful way to contribute to solving a world-wide issue.

The Peace Corps is very structured. It includes language training beforehand, a matchup to a place where Annie could make a major contribution, and a couple years of very hard work. Annie certainly has a wide range of skills and experience that she could contribute if she had the commitment to participate.

The Peace Corps is a paid volunteer program. Like many other volunteering programs, it takes people of all ages. If Annie went, she would meet people of all ages and have the experience of a lifetime without spending down her savings.

There are of course many other volunteer programs overseas for

Annie, including opportunities in teaching, healthcare, economic and agricultural aid, archeology and many other areas. Some are paid but most are not. Some you have to pay for yourself. Many programs have free time that you can use to explore the culture when you are not working.

TRIP STYLES AND ARRANGEMENTS

There are various styles of travel. Perhaps you have a partner to travel with. But maybe you do not, or your partner is unwilling or unable to go with you. If you travel solo, some outfits offer singles-only and singles-and-couples tours.

A key difference between travelling while working and while retired is that you can probably choose when during the year you want to go. You can avoid the periods when certain places are most crowded. You can use your time flexibility particularly if you are planning an unguided trip. Such travel can be less expensive and more fluid than going on guided tours.

If you go somewhere on your own, you might plan as much as possible how to get there, where to stay, and what to do, as well as arranging for day tours once you arrive. Or perhaps you will make lodging arrangements upon arrival and then ask around to learn what the locals recommend you see and do.

If your travel involves luxury, being catered to, then of course you will pay more. If the luxury trip is a package deal, then it is typically a take-it-or-leave-it proposition with little sightseeing or culture-sampling latitude.

Guided tours, even though more expensive and less flexible, have some advantages you may value:

- All the arrangements are made, including the logistics. Your guides know the local language and customs. Depending on your outlook, this can be a more efficient way to spend your traveling time.

- Tours offer the opportunity to meet people and make new friends.
- Some tours give you the chance to reinforce existing relationships, for example, by bringing family or friends along. And some tours are sponsored by faith communities, schools, charities, or other organizations.
- Education/learning may be enhanced led by a local tour guide who shares personal stories, history, and local lore. Guides can make places come alive.

There are hybrid approaches, with some aspects guided and others not. For example, there are self-guided hiking or biking tours in which an organization makes your rooming arrangements and gives you a map to get from place to place. Or someone will pick you up in the morning and drive you to the starting place of that day's hike.

Cruises have become especially popular over the last few decades. They offer a wide range of orientations:

- destinations: oceans versus rivers (and regions of the world to travel in) as well as themed trips.
- the amount of activity: off-boat excursions for the adventurous or on-board activities for the more mobility restricted.
- boat sizes: with tradeoffs for intimacy vs. more entertainment options
- accommodations: varying levels of luxury, with their associated costs
- pricing: à la carte or all-inclusive.

TRIP ACTIVITIES

Some trips center on a specific location or area, such as a national park, a region, or a country. Their activities mostly involve moving about and seeing the sites.

There are also trips oriented to a particular subject matter. These could include one focused on Elizabethan writers during which you visit places where the authors lived and worked. Or trips to famed music festivals or theatrical events. Or ones that take you to World War II battlegrounds.

Some trips are oriented around physical activity. There are, for example, group and solo bicycle tours. Some of these tours enable you to get off the beaten track.

What can make subject-oriented trips meaningful is the chance they provide to develop and enrich your interest in a particular topic.

CHALLENGES TO DOING EXTENSIVE TRAVEL

Planning. Generally, traveling is nonroutine. So the time and money aspects need to be thought through, perhaps budgeted for.

Money. The biggest challenge for most people who want to travel extensively is coming up with the money, particularly for that special bucket list trip. Travel can be very expensive and therefore a potential budget-buster.

If you tease apart the cost components, you can better determine what you can control and what you cannot. This could make the difference between being able to go and not.

Planning for a trip on your own to determine just what you want to do and see adds an element of adventure, which can be a plus or a minus, depending on your attitude and how things actually work out. This approach requires you to put in more time researching via the Internet, getting brochures and books, possibly working with a travel agent, etc. For some people, time spent on planning a trip is an unwanted chore; for others, it is part of the excitement.

Here are varied approaches that can reduce costs.

- *Transportation.* Consider going during the less expensive off-season. If you do, make sure that activities you want to do will be available then. Also, some popular programs can sell out early, so be sure to sign up for your first choices well in advance. Look for discount airline flights or specials. "Off-brand" airlines operate worldwide that are not much publicized in the United States. Spend time on the Internet to find such airlines and their offerings.

If you have special skills, particularly as a lecturer or entertainer, you may be able to get a job on board a ship. Some ships even hire people to help out with grunt work.

Perhaps you can piggyback from a work or volunteer experience. If your organization does business aboard, perhaps it will send you on its dime.

- *Accommodations.* Sharing space reduces costs. Some hostels, which are not just for college students any more, are less expensive.

  Renting from an apartment owner, through services such as Airbnb or VRBO, can be less expensive than a hotel. Some volunteer programs overseas provide free housing as part of the deal.

  If your trip is a month or longer and you can use a single location as a base, you may be able to arrange to exchange houses with someone there. Or you can arrange to housesit for someone while they are away.

Physical limitations. Tour outfits such as Road Scholar designate the level of activity necessary to keep up with the group. This can be important if you have special limitations or expectations regarding how much activity you want. Some tours offer multiple activity levels in case one partner has needs that are substantially different from the other. There are also tours designed for seniors with physical restrictions and challenges.

If your mobility is very restricted and you find no tour that matches what you can and want to do, you do not have to stay home. You can hire an experienced personal guide who can work with you to make it happen.

Unexpected accident or illness. Travel insurance can reimburse your costs—all or partial, depending on how much of the trip you need to cancel. Like other insurance, this adds to the cost. But if you have to collect, it can make a huge difference.

DOUG TRAVELS WITH LITTLE MONEY

Doug's appetite for travel has increased through the years. But he has not done much of it because he has not had the money. Once, however, he was invited to accompany the local orchestra on a Far East tour. It was a highlight of his life.

He might use his solid relationship with the orchestra to find opportunities to perform in a variety of places where the ensemble travels. He could also audition to play with other groups elsewhere in the United States or even abroad.

Also, he could assemble a group comprised of himself, a pianist, and a violinist to play classical and show music on a cruise ship. This would mean getting paid and getting to travel at the same time.

Doug does not have to earn large sums from such experiences, but the income could make traveling more feasible for him. If his major goal over the next few years is to build up a retirement fund, he will have to evaluate carefully how traveling will help or hurt in achieving that goal.

PREPARING FOR TRAVEL IN RETIREMENT

To develop travel plans, start with your notions about what you want, and then ask friends and relatives about trips they have taken.

They will provide numerous ideas and perhaps motivate you to explore the possibilities.

Friends and relatives can help you decide not just where to go but also how to do your trip. Learn how they addressed matters of time, money and, where pertinent, physical limitation.

If you want to take trips that involve being on your own in non-English-speaking countries, you can start learning a relevant foreign language. Having even a limited vocabulary when you go can make a big difference.

5. Your Housing and Your Life

As you prepare for retirement, think seriously about where you want to live. Your home functions as both your residence and as a valuable financial asset that must be managed carefully. When you retire, a convenient location in relation to your workplace is irrelevant. This affords you greater freedom about where you will live, but your choices will have significant implications. If, for example, you contemplate moving, remember that this decision will require major expenditures of time, energy, and money. But now that you will have more time to plan thoughtfully, you could choose to make it happen.

YOUR HOME AS A LOCATION

The structure you live in will determine the quality of your life during retirement. How will your home support your new lifestyle? To answer that question, review the following points.

Proximity to family and friends. How much time do you want to spend with your family and friends? Where are they located? How close to them do you need and/or want to be? Before making plans to move close to loved ones, be sure to find out how long they plan to remain where they presently live. After all, your children, nieces, and nephews could be at a stage in life when they intend to move for professional reasons.

Proximity to activities. Will your home be close to facilities you will be frequenting? What activities will you be doing and how often? Are there advantages in being close by? For example, do you want to live within driving distance of mountains, oceans, lakes, national parks, etc.? Is there a region of the country where you have always wanted to live?

Climate. Doubtless, you've heard some people say, "I just can't live in this climate anymore?" Is that person you?

Pace of lifestyle. Do you want to change the *pace* of your life as well as the *place* where you live? Which of these settings has more appeal: rural, urban, or suburban? Do you want to drive less often and far every day? Is this important enough that it determines where you want to live?

Size of housing. Is your home the right size and design to facilitate your optimal activities, including accommodations for relatives and friends when they come to visit? If your current home is too big to maintain and you want to downsize, are you thinking about owning a condominium or even renting? Have you considered getting some professional household help with chores and maintenance rather than moving to a smaller residence? If your current house isn't large enough for your projected retirement lifestyle, could you expand the space, or would it be practical to find a different home?

Services needed. Do you have a health situation that limits your mobility or requires the provision of special services? Many residential apartment communities, including senior-housing complexes, provide a variety of services, including meals in a common space, laundry, housecleaning, and various social and educational activities. Is this important at this stage of your life?

The average age of senior-housing residents is eighty-four; although some facilities accept residents aged fifty-five to sixty-five, most seniors move into them when they are somewhat older.

The process of selling a house is difficult for many people, who worry about a loss of privacy and fear they might be taken advantage of. It is possible to sell a home without putting it on the real estate market. A licensed realtor can provide useful guidance during this process.

Change. After selling your house and preparing to move, consider hiring a professional service to help sort through and dispose of your excess belongings.

Going to a new location means disconnecting from neighbors, friends, faith community, and doctors, among others, and establishing new relationships. Would this be an onerous chore or an exciting adventure for you?

One way to approach changing where you live is to try out the alternatives before making a decision. For example, if you are thinking about living in Oregon during retirement, consider visiting there several times for at least a month, and, if possible, at different times during the year. Renting a home or staying at an Airbnb or VRBO rather than renting a hotel room would more closely resemble the experience of actually living in a different locale.

BECKY'S DREAMS OF A DIFFERENT LIFE

Brian and Becky are sixty-four. Becky has just retired from her teaching job. Brian may or may not continue working after the two of them figure out if they can live comfortably on a single income, or one that is "fixed." Their kids are grown and living elsewhere, but within driving distance. Their house is larger than they really need or want to take care of.

Brian and Becky have long talked about the harsh climate where they live. It is too cold, and they love hot weather. When Brian retires, should they move to a warmer climate where they can spend more time outdoors all year?

Becky is fluent in Spanish, and Brian knows a little. Her dream has long been to live in a Spanish-speaking country. Is that feasible? Many Americans live abroad on a fixed income—their pensions and Social Security. Because Brian and Becky want to spend time with their children and grandchildren, living so far away from them will entail expensive travel. They may, therefore, want to include extra travel expenses in their future budget. As an alternative, they could consider living in the southern United States, which is also warm and much closer to family.

Even if the couple finds the perfect place abroad and move there, they might not want to sell their U.S. home immediately. At least in theory, they could rent it out for a while to help with the cash flow and move back into it if they later chose to.

YOUR HOME AS AN ASSET

Paying off your mortgage. Your home mortgage is probably your asset with the single largest loan against it. Many preretirees plan to pay off that loan around the time they retire. Should you do the same when you retire? There are a couple of ways to think about this.

First, there is the sense of security you might get from having no mortgage. Your monthly expenses would be greatly reduced, but you would still have to pay your property taxes and home insurance, which might have been bundled into your monthly payments. Having lower monthly expenses means drawing less from your investments and other sources of income. For many people, this is reason enough to pay off their mortgages.

Paying *down* the mortgage by making extra or larger monthly payments but not paying it *off* altogether won't reduce your future monthly expenses; it will, however, decrease the number of months you will need to make payments.

Does it make sense, then, from a financial perspective, to pay off the mortgage early? The answer depends on two factors: the interest rate on your mortgage and the source of the funds used to pay it off. The interest rate you are paying could be much less than you think when you take taxes into account. If you are itemizing deductions on your tax return, which is less likely under the 2017 tax-reform law but still possible, then the interest component of your mortgage is deductible. For example, if the interest rate on your mortgage is 4.5 percent and your marginal tax rate is 33 percent, then you can deduct 33 percent of 4.5 percent. The net cost of your mortgage is only 3 percent. From a financial standpoint, it makes sense to cash in an investment paying less than 3 percent to eliminate the 3 percent cost, but not an investment growing at a faster rate.

So, if you have surplus cash on hand, you could profitably use it to pay off the mortgage. If bonds are paying only nominal interest because interest rates are very low, then they could be cashed in and used to pay off the mortgage. It probably would not be profitable in the long run to cash in stocks unless mortgage rates were in the double-digit range.

Your most expensive source of money for paying off the mortgage is your IRA or other pretax retirement plan. Like other distributions from retirement plans, 100 percent of the money you receive will be taxable. Don't cash it in. You'll be much better off postponing taxable distributions as long as possible.

Ultimately, paying off your mortgage does *not* make you much better off financially. You are eliminating mortgage payments in return for reducing future income from the account cashed in. The differences between the two cash-flow streams should be minimal. And by taking money out of cash and putting it into home equity, you reduce flexibility by tying up that money in your house.

Instead of paying down the mortgage, consider improving the

condition of your house before retirement so you won't need the money to pay for repairs or upgrades after retiring. Where the money comes from for these projects will affect your future cash flow, just as it will for paying off your mortgage.

Using your home to help make ends meet. If you want to stay in your home but are having trouble making ends meet, you might consider using the residence to decrease your household expenses or increase your income, or both. If your children have moved out of the house and their rooms are empty and unused, you could rent out the rooms on a long-term basis. Or you could rent them out through Airbnb or a similar service. Among the trade-offs are some extra work and loss of privacy in exchange for the extra cash.

Home sharing is another option, particularly if you use only part of a large house and are willing to rent out the rest to someone else. A renter might be willing to provide some basic care services in return for a bedroom, bathroom, parking, and access to the kitchen. If your home is large enough, you could have more than one tenant, and they could split the work.

If you own more land than you need or use, you might consider adding on to your home or even building a small dwelling on the property, assuming local building codes would permit this. You could then rent that space to generate income or to house someone who could provide services to you.

Tapping into your home equity. The first way is to sell your home, buy a less expensive one, and pocket the difference. You can use the freed-up money in order to generate income, pay off debt, or gift it to others.

A second way is to sell your home and then rent a different place to live. You could then invest all the proceeds from the home sale and use the investment income, and maybe some of the principal, to pay the rent. This is as much a lifestyle change as it is a financial one. Rents may increase because of inflation, but not investment income, so this approach might be more practical over a shorter period of years than over several decades.

The third way is to set up a home equity credit line (HECL) with a bank, generally with the one holding your mortgage. This arrangement allows you to request a cash advance from the bank whenever you need it. Before the housing bubble burst in 2007 and 2008, some people used their HECL as an ATM machine, believing that home prices could only rise, and that they could use the increasing equity to live beyond their means. But when home prices dropped, they found themselves "under water." A loan is not free—it accrues interest. Some banks require you to pay back the HECL within ten years, although you may be able to renew it.

An HECL can work well if used properly, particularly if you need cash for a short period and are then able to pay off the loan. Be sure to check the closing costs for setting up an HECL; they may be less than for setting up a new mortgage or for a full refinancing, but they still could be substantial.

The fourth way to tap your home equity is through a reverse mortgage from a bank. If you have substantial equity in your home and are over sixty-five, a reverse mortgage will provide you with either a lump sum to invest and spend, a credit line to use later for the same purpose, or a regular stream of money for as long as you and your spouse or partner live and remain in the same home. As long as you continue to pay for home insurance and property taxes, the bank cannot kick you out of your home, no matter how long you live.

Here is how a reverse mortgage works. The bank uses your age or ages to estimate your life expectancy. It will give you only enough money so the bank can recoup its costs, which include any money it has given you plus the interest it needs to receive on the mortgage. When you leave your home—either by moving or dying—the bank settles up. If this happens shortly after you've taken out the reverse mortgage and there is substantial unused money, the bank recoups its costs and pays the difference to you or your heirs. If you stay in your home for a long time, any residual equity will be used up. The bank then owns and can sell the home to pay itself back, leaving you without a home to pass on to your heirs.

The trade-off with a reverse mortgage is that you give up some of your heirs' future inheritance in return for a pool or stream of money during your lifetime.

There are substantial closing costs with a reverse mortgage, frequently twice those of a typical mortgage. Getting one should be an action of last resort, but it may be necessary, particularly if you spend down all your assets/investments and have to rely only on Social Security. If your home equity is the only asset you have, you can use a reverse mortgage to supplement your income and lifestyle—and never again make conventional mortgage payments.

The tax implications of selling your home. If you have lived in your primary residence for two of the last five years before selling it, then $250,000, or $500,000 per couple, of capital gains is not taxed. Be sure to keep track of any capital improvements you've made on the house through the years, because you can subtract those costs from any gains when calculating the taxes due.

YOUR HOME AS BOTH A LOCATION AND AN ASSET

Some people own more than one home. The two most common examples are a vacation property or a time-share. A second home could also be a place to live part-time in, say, a larger city or a warmer climate during winter. Retirement might be a time to consider adding one to your assets because owning property is often a sound investment. Some people say that buying their home was the best financial decision they ever made, now that the property is worth much more than what they paid for it. If their mortgage payments were not much higher than their rent payments would have been, then homeownership probably worked out quite well for them.

But what if your mortgage payments are much higher than rental costs for an equivalent property? And what if you had rented instead of buying a house and invested the extra money in investments? Stock investments have historically grown at a much faster rate than real estate value, so theoretically, buying stocks would have been the wiser option. Of course, the intangible benefits of owning your home may well be much more important to you.

Think about the ownership of a second home more as an enhancement to your standard of living than as an investment. If, however, it is part of your retirement plan, remember to consider transaction expenses—realtor and mortgage-setup costs—when buying another house. From a financial standpoint, owning a home rather than renting will work out much better if you plan to live there at least two to five years.

If you want to stay in your home most of the time but spend part of each year at a different location, you can rent another place each year or you can own one. Renting has the advantage of flexibility: you can go to different places at different times. Furthermore, you are not responsible for managing the place where you stay when you are away from the home you own. For instance, you can leave your belongings in your second home and just go there to enjoy it.

Maintaining a second property can require considerable time and even physical labor. If your second property is a condominium, remember that the condo association can raise its fees or even assess you for necessary property repair if it is not making ends meet.

In theory, you can rent a second home out when you are not there in order to recoup some of the expenditures or even to make some extra money. Doing so is on par with running a small business. It entails finding and screening renters, collecting the rent, maintaining the property, and even repairing damage done by renters. There are, of course, management companies that will handle the day-to-day work for you, for a price, but the property is ultimately your responsibility. Owning it is more about enhancing your lifestyle than making a savvy investment, especially if you don't use it often enough to justify the expenditures of time and money.

CHALLENGES IN HOUSING

Housing costs of all kinds will most likely be the second largest component of your retirement budget, second only to taxes. Smart choices in this area will have a significant effect on your standard of living and your ability to afford and enjoy your preferred retirement activities. The stakes are high.

The cost of making a change in housing can be substantial, not just in dollars but in time. You may need to sort through decades of accumulated belongings, especially if you are moving to a smaller residence. You will need to make countless decisions about what to keep and move, give away, sell or throw out.

The quality of your life after moving will probably depend as much on your relationships with neighbors and community as on the features of the structure itself. That is difficult to know initially and can change over time. Some research supports the theory that the most important assets in your life are your networks. Consider that the automotive pioneer Henry Ford lost everything in a fire that burned down his factories, but his network of employees and friends stuck with him and helped him rebuild. If you move far away, will you be able to maintain relationships with established networks or replace them if you can't?

For married or cohabiting couples, a major challenge is agreeing about where to live. After all, two people planning to live together during retirement could have different notions of where and how they want to spend their time. Because some locations have more advantages for one person than the other, this issue should be resolved prior to a move.

PREPARING FOR A DIFFERENT HOUSING ARRANGEMENT

Your home can provide you with huge opportunities for a better life. Changes in housing may even help you accomplish multiple objectives, e.g. a better location, size and cash flow at the same time.

To a large extent where you live will depend on what you want to do during retirement. So any planning you do about the activities during your retirement will be a step in the right direction. Get started thinking and researching early, because it will take some time to explore the options, make decisions and act on them. Researching the alternatives will be essential.

6. Love and Support

A key feature of a successful retirement is a positive relationship with your partner. At their best, such relationships can provide emotional support to both you and your partner and can nurture feelings of love and connection rather than loneliness and isolation.

CHALLENGES IN LEAVING WORK

The most obvious immediate challenge to be faced when you retire is the loss of your earned income. Somewhat less obvious but still profound is the loss of frequent and enjoyable socializing with your coworkers. You may continue seeing some of them after you retire, but if they are still working, you will have to adjust your schedule with theirs.

Furthermore, you will miss the organizational structure your job provided, whether or not you liked that job. It may even have given your life a sense of purpose.

For some people, retiring means a loss of status and self-definition. They may even feel as though they no longer have an identity.

To adjust to the losses of relationships and structure that retirees face, some use their newfound time to develop relationships with others. Sharing your experience can add purpose and meaning to your retirement years. Positive interactions with past coworkers, a partner, your family, friends, and community can help you adjust to your new life.

SUPPORT FROM YOUR PARTNER

A partner can provide understanding particularly if your relationship is strong. A supportive partner can help ease your adjustment to the losses you will no doubt experience. Sometimes, a partnership is strengthened in retirement. Undoubtedly, your relationship will change when you have more free, unstructured time; therefore, adjustments in your relationship with your partner are inevitable. Unfortunately, there is the possibility that the relationship could weaken and even end after you retire. But if it is strong, it is also possible that you and your partner will grow even closer.

Now that retirees are typically living longer, there is a small but growing trend for people in their fifties and beyond to separate or divorce if their marriage or relationship is troubled. Money is only one factor that drives couples to split. Sometimes, individuals crave more independence or a better quality of life. Some people going through divorce describe their reason as being their last chance to get it right.

Repartnering after death or divorce is generally challenging. First of all, there is of course the matter of finding the right person. Some hesitate to remarry because of health problems or a lack of confidence. Some retirees choose to live with a new partner rather than remarry. Remarriage can be more difficult for women than for men. Because women typically live longer and men frequently choose younger wives, there are fewer older men available for older women; in fact, there are more than ten times the number of widows in the United States than widowers. Proof of this disparity is that 60 percent of older men remarry, but only 20 percent of older women do. Men who remarry do so within an average of two years of losing a spouse to death or divorce, whereas the comparable number for women is three to five years.

A key advantage of being part of a couple is the provision of mutual practical support—as in helping each other perform the routine tasks. If both individuals are fully physically functional, they can share much of the household work and be there for each other during health crises.

When one of you becomes sick or dies, your sharing arrangement may change radically. You might have to assume responsibilities that formerly were your partner's. If so, you may confront new challenges. For example, do you know what monthly bills need to be paid, if your partner used to do that? What and where are your investments? How about essential passwords?

Obviously, it is vital that each of you in a couple relationship has the skills to be a backup for the other or, at least, to have a plan for what you will do when your current circumstances change.

SUPPORT FROM YOUR FAMILY: ADULT CHILDREN, GRANDCHILDREN, SIBLINGS, AND OTHER RELATIVES

No, you didn't choose them and, yes, you have had a long history in your relationships with them. You might be very close to some of them but not to others. Some family members will be eager to supply you with love and support in retirement, just as you might want to provide those same things to them. Others may not be part of your support network at all.

Regardless of the state of each relationship, there remains the notion that "blood is thicker than water," that you will be there for each other in tough times. Realistically, of course, that might not actually happen to be the case. Will one or more of your children be available and interested in providing help when you really need it? Have they seen how you have helped and respected your own parents, a model they may want to follow?

Your relationships with family members depend on several factors. One is the quality of your past interactions. Another is your proximity to them; living nearby makes frequent interactions easier, but only if you get along well. And then there is the age difference.

Positive family relationships facilitate general feelings of mutual love and a willingness to provide love and support for each other. Relationships that have been challenging or difficult have the potential to change for the better. Retirement might be the right time to work on improving these relationships. Sometimes, the health challenges or death of one relative can change everything in your relationship with other family members. This kind of change in circumstances may be an opportunity for you to draw closer.

The benefits of improved relationships can be substantial. Your siblings, for example, shared the experience of growing up with you; learning their perspective on your early family interactions can provide valuable insights into how you developed as an adult.

SUE AND HER FAMILY WORK TOGETHER ON FAMILY ISSUES

Sue, the ninety-year-old matriarch of the Miller family, is still living independently in her own home. Family is everything to her. She would like to see her children and grandchildren more often, and hopes that the relationships among her children and their families will remain strong when she is no longer around to encourage them. Sue has several chronic health conditions—arthritis, diabetes, and congestive heart failure—but so far, she has been able to manage them on her own. She realizes that she may need more care in the future, and worries that her money might run out over the next few years. Sue has never shared information about her financial status with any of her children, who now wonder if they eventually will have to help their mother financially.

One route to opening up communication about situations such as Sue's is to hold a family meeting. The key to assuring that such a meeting is successful is to encourage participation by all involved family members, who should listen carefully to one another and be mutually respectful. Here are some agenda items for Sue and her family to consider as part of their anticipated discussion:

- Sue's current financial situation and expectations for the future, as described by Sue herself or a trusted advisor. Participants should have access to relevant documents and a proposed budget, if possible.
- Sue's current health status and expectations for her future health care.
- Information about the status and location of her legal documents, including her will, powers of attorney, and beneficiaries.
- Plan for the disposition of her personal property. Sue can handle this sometimes sensitive issue in one of three ways. She can make a list of items and the heirs for each and attach the list to her will. She can ask family members to identify what they want and put their names on the items. Or she can bring the family together and ask them all to take turns choosing their preferred items.

If there is an anticipation that such a meeting might be highly emotional or even rancorous, a neutral facilitator could be present to moderate it. If there are disagreements when the issues are discussed, there will be time to work them out in circumstances less stressful than immediately after Sue's eventual death.

SUPPORT FROM YOUR FRIENDS

Friends can be as close as family, sometimes even closer, and are particularly important when you have no partner or family nearby. To derive the maximum benefit of friendships, which are not dependent on family ties, they must be nurtured, or you and your friends may drift apart. Aging presents challenges for friendships, which can change over time. Some of your friends may concentrate solely on their own families instead of finding time for you. Some may move away or die. These changes can create instability, a sense of loss, and sometimes even depression.

SUPPORT FROM YOUR COMMUNITY

Communities can be an important source of support because they bring people together for various reasons.

- Communities of interest. A faith community, for example, includes people who want to share religious ideas and activities with others who believe as they do.
- Neighbors, the people who live nearby and with whom you might want to interact frequently, or at least occasionally.
- Professional groups. These consist of employees at your former workplace or people who share the same profession.
- Social-action groups, including political groups and those organized to foster change.

Participation in a community can be an antidote to loneliness. Although the purpose of a community is not to support its individual members, very often those members do become friends. Because a successful community survives the life spans of its individual members, you will be able to form new friendships even when some members drop out, move away, or die.

Another way for retirees to be part of a community is to live in senior housing. This option becomes more desirable as you age, because some facilities provide such services as meal preparation, housekeeping, and basic healthcare. Those communities called "continuing care" may offer independent-living apartments for seniors and also provisions for more advanced medical care as needed.

Before you consider this possible route, find out the average age of the people living in the given community; you might—or might not—want to live with people who are approximately your age.

If you move to housing in a different town, where you don't know anyone who also lives there, you should have a plan for reaching out and establishing new connections and, eventually, friendships.

- Join an existing group oriented around activities that you have enjoyed doing in the past, such as singing in a chorus or participating in a photography, art, or writing group.
- Join a faith community, whether or not you belonged to one.
- Join a service organization such as the Knights of Columbus, Elks, or Rotarians and volunteer to help.

Paid professionals can help you resolve problems in various ways. If, for example, you are having significant problems interacting with family members and you want to change and improve those relationships, a therapist could be helpful, maybe even essential.

PREPARING FOR CHANGES IN RELATIONSHIPS IN RETIREMENT

Building relationships that will continue beyond your working life and developing capabilities to support others you will be spending time with are two imperatives to consider before you retire.

As for building relationships and intimacy, remember the concept of *entropy*, the law of physics that says things fall apart unless you apply resources to hold them together. For relationships, those resources include time, energy, creativity, good will, and maybe even love. Another constructive way to think about building intimacy is to picture an emotional bank: you must make deposits before you can take withdrawals. Those deposits, which can be made before or after you retire, include time together, empathy, listening, understanding, respecting, validating, and providing warmth and affection.

Developing capabilities to support others and be supported yourself is the second way to prepare for dealing with relationships in retirement. Consider, for example, the daunting task of assuming care for your spouse or partner, especially if this transition occurs suddenly and unexpectedly. It may require learning new caretaking skills, hiring others to help, or drawing on your relationships with family and friends.

Preparations for relationships in retirement can begin before or after you retire. But you will probably have more time afterward. One place to start is the organization of your affairs—that is, documenting how you contribute to your relationships and where you store critical information. Let's say you start organizing your finances by making a list of accounts, amounts of each, the income they generate, and their passwords. Under certain circumstances, that list can prove to be valuable to you and others. Where you store this information is critical. Using your computer has the advantage of safe maintenance of the list. A paper list could be lost or destroyed. Whoever will need to use the list must know that it exists, where it is located, and if the information is digital or on paper. The list of your finances has to be so secure that hackers or other crooks cannot gain access to it.

Any time you spend transferring information will be well spent. Your partner and others in your life eventually will thank you for it.

Meanwhile, before you retire, nurture and cherish positive relationships with family and friends.

7. Blood and Money

As you approach retirement, you may have more financial capital than your children or your parents. Perhaps you have it, and they want it. The conversation may start with their asking you for money, or maybe you can start it by offering to help them.

Giving money to relatives, or not giving it, can be complicated because it is much more than about money per se and can trigger various emotions regarding expectations and past personal history. It can foster resentments, dependency, anxiety, or depression, or it can relieve financial stress and help people get closer to one another. In other words, tread carefully when weighing decisions about giving money to others.

If you are the gifter/donor, you may want to consider money transfers as part of budgeting for your retirement. Having enough money after you retire means you won't be dependent on the largess of parents or children. If you die before having spent all your money, others will have to determine how to transfer what remains to your family or others. (The tax rules concerning transferring during your lifetime and after death are addressed in Chapter 8.)

GIVING TO FAMILY MEMBERS

One meaningful way you can help family members is to give them money for which you expect no repayment. Called gifting, this approach can have substantial consequences both for you and the recipients. Here are some reasons why you may want to gift money to your family:

- To supplement their income from a low-paying job. For example, a family member might earn no or little income for a variety of reasons. Perhaps he or she works in the arts, which frequently aren't lucrative, or the individual works part-time while getting professional training.

- To provide a business loan that, ideally, would assist the recipient in earning a future livelihood. Remember, however, that most fledgling businesses fail, meaning that the loan recipient may not be able to pay you back.

- To help pay off the costs of a serious medical problem.

- To supplement school-tuition costs. Private school can be expensive, even at the preschool and elementary level. If you want to help a relative pay for post-high school training by putting the money aside in advance, you can make contributions to a 529 or other college-funding plan. Such plans have one owner and one beneficiary, such as a grandchild; you or your adult son or daughter can be the owner and thus can make decisions about disbursements for college and change the beneficiary when appropriate. A 529 and other college-savings plans for children and grandchildren permit growth of investments without ever being taxed, as long as the money is used for approved post-secondary education.

- To pay for special activity programs such as in the arts, sports, or religious training.

- To give simply because you can and want to be generous, or perhaps because you want your children to have more money and options than you did when you were their age. Providing financial help to adult children, grandchildren, and other family members is voluntary and discretionary in our society. As you consider doing so and as you prepare for your own retirement, be sure you understand exactly what you can and cannot afford to give. After all, you do not want to exhaust your own assets and then become dependent on your children or other relatives.

CATHY AND CHUCK WANT TO HELP THEIR SON, DAUGHTER-IN-LAW, AND GRANDCHILDREN

Cathy and Chuck's youngest son, Cody, is a professional cellist. He will never get involved in the management of his parents' restaurant, but he does work there part-time. Cody's wife, Rona, is an aspiring writer. The couple has trouble earning enough to support themselves and their two young children. They live in a small apartment in a questionable part of town. Cathy and Chuck feel they should step in by helping Cody and Rona acquire more  adequate housing that won't burden them with large mortgage payments. Instead of cosigning on a home loan, they can make a substantial down payment on a house. After the couple finds a suitable

 small house, Cathy and Chuck can arrange for a mortgage in their own names; they would then own the home and could charge the kids a modest but fair rent. If they choose, they could also give Cody and Rona enough money to pay the rent.

There are other ways they could help. If Cathy and Chuck want

Cody and Rona to develop their own good credit rating, they could set up a credit or debit card for the children with a low credit limit to use in their own names. Then the parents could make the regular monthly payments.

TAX CONSEQUENCES OF MAKING GIFTS

Whether you make gifts before or during retirement, it is important to know the tax implications of such gifts, because you, the donor, not the recipient, are the one who pays the taxes. Any and all gifts you make are subject to gift taxes—with the following five exceptions:

1. Gifts of any size to a spouse.
2. Gifts of any size to recognized charities. Gifts to political lobbying organizations might not qualify.
3. Small annual gifts. In 2018 these are defined as less than $15,000 per donor per recipient. For example, if you and your partner want to maximize gifts to your three grandchildren, the two of you can gift $30,000 to each grandchild each calendar year without paying any gift taxes or filing federal tax forms. Because 529 educational plans have a special provision that permits you to gift ahead by up to four years, you and your spouse could conceivably could each gift up to $75,000 in the first year for each of your grandchildren without incurring a gift tax unless you die within four years of making the donation.
4. "Small" lifetime gifts in addition to the annual gifts. The limit for untaxed lifetime gifts, above and beyond the annual gifts, was doubled in 2018, under the new tax-reform law to $11,180,000 per donor—for federal gift taxes. Some but not all states have a gift tax in addition to the federal tax; the limits for these can be substantially lower. Minnesota, for example, taxes lifetime gifts greater than $2,400,000 per person for people dying in 2018. Whenever your annual gift is

greater than the annual limit and you want to use up some of your lifetime limit, be sure to file the appropriate tax forms.

5. Direct payments to a school for tuition or to a healthcare provider, even if the education or healthcare is for someone else. Note, however, that a gift to a child who then uses that money to pay tuition or medical bills is subject to gift tax.

TACTICS FOR REDUCING TAXES WHEN GIFTING

You can spread out a gift over several years. For example, if you give money to a child to purchase a car, you can make your first car payment in one calendar year and the second in the following year. If the gift is too large to be paid for in two years, you can make a loan to the recipient, who must pay it back to you. If desired, you can then forgive future loan payments over a period of time. The forgiven amounts for principal and interest on the loan are then transformed into gifts. If the forgiven amounts are less than the annual limits, no taxes are due. Your attorney and accountant will help you prepare this legal document, officially called a SCIN (self-canceling investment note).

If you make very substantial gifts to parents or children of any age for their living expenses, you may be entitled to deduct these recipients as dependents when filing your income taxes, assuming you provide more than half their support. If you are sharing the gifting with someone else, one of you may be able to take the deduction one year and the other take the deduction the following year.

Needless to say, gifting can get complicated, so if you plan to make substantial gifts, you should take tax laws into account and discuss them with your accountant or financial planner.

INVOLVING OTHERS IN THE MANAGEMENT OF YOUR FINANCIAL AFFAIRS

There are two frequently used types of legal documents that allow family members to be involved in managing your money without receiving an outright gift from you. One is a trust and the other is a power of attorney; both can help you manage your financial affairs while you are still alive.

A trust is a legal document with a set of instructions that directs the trustee regarding the disbursement of income and principal assets held by the trust. It is often used to give money to family members, usually but not necessarily upon your death. It serves to protect your money from being handled and invested by inexperienced beneficiaries. It protects the money from creditors, and even from an ex-spouse if you are going through a divorce.

There are several types of trusts. A revocable, or living, trust lets you, the trustee, put assets into your trust and remove them whenever you want while you are alive and competent. Trusts have a provision for managing the assets if you are unable to do so yourself.

Powers of attorney (POAs) are straightforward legal documents that give someone else the ability to sign documents and make financial arrangements for you. Without a POA, you run the risk of having the courts appoint a guardian to make decisions for you if you cannot make them yourself. No wonder some people believe that POAs are every bit as important as wills.

There are two general types of POAs, and you, your parents, and your children should have both. One, called a durable POA, deals with financial management, even if you cannot do it yourself. The other is a healthcare POA, which gives someone else the authority to make medical decisions for you should you become incapable of doing so yourself.

Every POA document should specify both a primary and a contingent, or secondary, person with the legal power to make critical decisions. If more than one person has that power, you decide if either person can make decisions or if both people are required. Keep in mind that the person with the POA can have considerable control of your finances.

Even though the POA is a legal document, it is frequently written in a standardized way. In fact, some states have passed statutes spelling out the exact wording to be used in a POA. If so, you may be able to obtain the so-called statutory form from a stationery store or via the Internet, and you can ask your attorney for help as you prepare the forms as part of your estate planning. A notary must witness your signature after you complete one or both types of POA. If you want to have sole control over your money as long as possible, you may not want to relinquish your POA document immediately to the person to whom you are granting the power. However, it is critical that you tell that individual that the POA exists and where it is being stored for safekeeping.

You must be "of sound mind" when you sign any legal agreements such as this. Thus waiting until you really need the POA could be too late to prepare it. Since there is the unfortunate possibility that you won't be "of sound mind" as you age, it is particularly important to have this in place while your mind is indeed sound. But it is important at any age because of life's uncertainties.

PREPARING TO HELP FAMILY IN RETIREMENT

Substantial giving is potentially the biggest budget buster of them all. It is very important for you to have a good understanding of what you can and cannot afford.

Your preparation in this area for retirement is threefold:

- Include gifting in your retirement budget if you expect to be making gifts.
- Set up your own powers-of-attorney now, or as part of any estate planning that you are doing soon.
- Consider setting up trusts as part of your future money management.

8. The Hereafter

There are many reasons why now, as you plan for retirement, may be the right time to review and perhaps make changes to your estate planning.

- You may originally have done your estate planning long ago.
- Your family, health, and/or work circumstances may have changed.
- You may have very different ideas about how you want your estate handled after your death.
- You now likely have a realistic attitude toward mortality and an acceptance of the fact that "you can't take it with you."
- You may have witnessed the results of successful or unsuccessful estate planning for your parents or other relatives or friends.
- If you have successfully managed your money so far and continue to do so during retirement, you may well have a considerable amount to pass on. A larger estate may be the result of
  - the growth of your savings and investments over time,
  - an inheritance,

- funds remaining in an emergency buffer built up to deal with, say, healthcare expenses, and
- your house, if you still have one.

A challenge in working on your estate plan is deciding how best to distribute the funds. What if you have more than one offspring and their circumstances are quite different from one another? For example, one child or grandchild might have serious health problems and future expenses but not the other children. Do you give more to the individual who needs it the most? Or what if one child is far more financially successful than the others? Do you give that one less? Or if you have already made substantial monetary gifts to one child, do you give more in your estate to the others to make up for the share they missed? Or what if you like one child less than the others? Do you arrange to leave him or her less of your estate or even nothing at all?

Answers to each of these questions have financial ramifications as well as psychological ones. Is an equal distribution the same as a fair one? There is no single right answer to any of these questions, and you may well have different ideas from others you know. You must decide what is right for you. As the circumstances for you and your beneficiaries evolve, you can imagine working quite closely and productively with your estate planning attorney.

WILLS

Do you currently have an outdated will, or an up-to-date will, or no will at all? In truth, *everyone* has a will. Even if you die intestate (seemingly without a will), your state of residence has one for you, but how it distributes your estate might not be what you would have desired.

If you have a will, does it accomplish what you want it to? This seemingly simple question may be difficult to answer because the actual document is written in technical "legalese."

The most straightforward version is sometimes called a simple, or "I love you," will. It legally leaves everything to your partner, if you have one; if you don't, your estate goes to your living children in equal shares or, if they are deceased, to *their* children. In this situation, your offspring are your secondary, or contingent, heirs.

BENEFICIARIES

Any asset you own that has a beneficiary will override your will when you die. That is, it will go directly to your stipulated beneficiaries. The most common accounts that have beneficiaries are IRAs of all kinds, retirement plans such as 401(k)s, life insurance, annuities, trusts, jointly held accounts, and accounts payable on death (POD). It is critical to make sure beneficiary accounts are compatible with your will and that they designate both primary and contingent beneficiaries properly.

TRUSTS

Revocable living trusts, which you create and use during your lifetime, also determine what happens to assets held by your trust after your death. Sometimes described as will substitutes, revocable living trusts direct what happens only to assets owned by that particular trust. Testamentary trusts, which are included in and created by your will upon your death, are another approach to holding and directing money for your beneficiaries.

A "kiddie trust" is a revocable or testamentary trust set up to manage assets for minor children, who are unable to manage money for themselves. It spells out what happens to the income and principal of the assets in the trust—for the benefit of the children. People who have children from several marriages typically use trusts in order to guarantee that children from a previous marriage, rather than just children from a current marriage, inherit assets held by the trust.

There are other kinds of more specialized instruments, such as special-needs trusts, which provide benefits to family members who require special care. If set up properly, the beneficiaries can collect some benefits from the trust while still being permitted to collect payments from social-service agencies. There are also types of trusts used in advanced estate planning, sometimes for wealthy people, that contain real estate or business interests.

BRIAN AND BECKY AND THEIR HIS/HER/OUR FAMILY

Brian and Becky have three sets of children—his, hers, and theirs—and they love them all. Their son Billy, born with birth defects, will always need specialized care, and his parents are thinking about how his needs will be met after they are gone. Treating family members fairly as opposed to equally is a matter of great concern to them. In the past, they have helped Becky's daughter, who was a single mother and could not support herself, and Brian's son, who needed money to start a business, but they have not helped Brian's daughter. They also want to leave some money to those grandchildren who are too young to manage an inheritance themselves. Now, they need something more than the "I love you" wills drawn up decades ago.

Billy, who can't take care of himself, depends on public assistance for his care and support. Brian and Becky currently provide money for whatever is not provided by governmental assistance. If they were to leave money directly to Billy after their deaths, he would no longer be eligible for government aid, and the inheritance would be quickly dissipated.

Instead, they could leave some of their inheritance to a special-needs trust, which would hold the money for Billy's benefit and keep him eligible for continued government help. It would also provide professional management of the money and protection against creditors.

However, they do not know how much of an inheritance there will be for Billy and the other children after they spend their retirement money. They could, of course, set up a trust soon and fund it with life insurance; this would allow them to transfer smaller amounts of money to the trust so the trustee can purchase a joint-and-survivor life insurance policy; as long as they continue paying the premiums, they guarantee that the money for Billy will be there when they are not.

There are two ways Brian and Becky can assure that their inheritance goes to the right people—with so-called soft wiring, or no trust, or with hard wiring a trust. The former means they can leave money to their children and request that they give a certain amount to the grandchildren. Or they can leave money in a "kiddie trust" (hard wiring), which controls when and how much money will go to the grandchildren. Either approach permits them to leave money for their adult children and grandchildren. If money is *not* left to a trust as a beneficiary when Brian or Becky dies, the survivor could change his or her will for the benefit of their biological child(ren) from a previous marriage, thereby excluding other children for the rest of the inheritance.

Brian and Becky want to be fair to all their children and leave them equal inheritances. They could calculate all the money they have already used to support two of their three children and subtract that from their shares of the inheritance. Whether that is fair or even equal is up to them. If they decide to proceed that way, they will have to be sure that their beneficiaries are aware of their parents' desires and decisions.

When Becky retires, she will probably be able to retain her life insurance only *if* she converts it to a much higher-premium policy that will cover her for the rest of her life. Such insurance is called whole life. As long as Becky has good health and is insurable elsewhere, the offer through work will generally be more expensive than other life insurance she could obtain elsewhere. If she and Brian have enough money to support both of them, they probably will have enough if only one of them is alive—as long as their retirement income does not disappear when one of them dies. Life insurance in retirement would not be to provide for the other spouse but to provide an inheritance to others, perhaps through a trust that owns the life insurance and distributes money to them.

PROBATE

Any bank or investment accounts you own that are jointly held or have a beneficiary go directly to the beneficiary upon your death. But if some of your assets lack a beneficiary—for example, your car and home—and are worth in total more than a token amount (e.g., $50,000), whether or not you have a will, your estate will go through probate to dispose of those assets. Probate is a public court process that requires the executor of your will or a court-appointed representative if you have no will to collect, catalog, and disperse non-beneficiary assets to your heirs. Such a process can cost up to 5 percent of the value of the assets, can take years to complete, and is public knowledge.

To avoid probate, you can transform your non-beneficiary assets into beneficiary ones in one of two ways. The first is to move the assets to your revocable living trust, if you have one. The second is to change the owner of the account from your name to your name plus POD (payable on death) and the name of your beneficiary. Sometimes TOD (transfer on death) is used instead. Showing a death certificate changes the owner of your assets to the beneficiary.

LIFE INSURANCE

Owning life insurance enables you to take care of your beneficiaries after your death. It is also an effective way to increase the size of your estate. The process is straightforward: you pay the premium to an insurance company and, after your death, the company pays a benefit to a beneficiary. A life insurance policy is a legal document and is considered a contract.

If you are retired and have accumulated enough assets to provide income for both you and your partner, there may well be enough money for a survivor without the need for a life insurance benefit. Although many people discontinue their life insurance policies upon retirement, there are valid reasons not to do so. For example, suppose you both are primarily living off Social Security and pensions; that income will be substantially reduced or eliminated when one of you dies. In that case, life insurance could replace at least some of the lost income for the surviving partner. Another reason to buy life insurance is to create an estate for your children or other family members, especially if you anticipate depleting your assets over your lifetime but still want money to be available to others upon your death.

If you want the death benefit to be paid out only after both you and your partner have died, you can purchase a "joint and survivor," or a "last-to-die," policy. Even if one of you is uninsurable because of health issues, it is still possible to obtain such a policy as long as the healthy partner is insurable. To do so is less expensive than buying separate policies for each partner.

The type of life insurance you choose also will depend on how long you want the policy to remain in place and when you want it to pay out. If your goal is to have the insurance for a term of years, then a term policy may work best. As you age, however, you probably want the insurance to remain in place for the rest of your life; in that case, a whole-life policy or some variant with cash values and guarantees would be more appropriate. The initial premiums will be more expensive initially because you are accumulating reserves for later. But it will be more affordable later on when mortality rates and premiums rise.

CATHY AND CHUCK PLAN FOR THEIR FAMILY AND BUSINESS

Chuck and Cathy have not done any estate planning since their kids were young because they did not know what to do regarding their

business, inheritance, and legacy. They do know they want to run the restaurant themselves for as long as they can and still keep it in the family in the future. Their daughter, Courtney, is their logical successor because she already does a great job working with her parents, and they believe she can eventually assume a leadership role. Their son Carl could also get more involved as he gets a little older and more experienced, but Cody, the other son, wants to focus on his career as a musician.

Although nearly all of Cathy and Chuck's assets are tied up in the restaurant, they do not know how much that business is worth. They want to treat their three children fairly and equitably, and could leave equal shares of the business to each of their children upon their deaths. But this approach could prove disastrous, because one inheritor who is uninvolved would receive as much control and benefit from the business as the one who is running it. A much better way to resolve this issue is to set up a life insurance policy through which each of those who are not inheriting the business gets a sum comparable to the restaurant's value. Or Courtney could buy a life insurance policy on her parents and then use the proceeds to buy out her siblings' shares of the business. In either case, if the business will be transferred after Chuck and Cathy have both died, the policy should be on both their lives.

Most likely, Cathy and Chuck will want to give some shares of the business to Courtney while they are still alive—as a reward for her good work and as an incentive for her to assume more responsibility. If so, they will have to calculate the value of such gifts, which, if they are too large, might require them to pay gift taxes.

Should Chuck and Cathy fully retire,

they could try giving the entire business to their children. But if they have no other investments to live off, how will they pay their bills? And if Courtney and Carl want to buy the business from their parents, they won't have the money to do so. They could, of course, take out a loan and pay their parents all at once. Or they might like to pay for the business over a period of time; if so, Cathy and Chuck should agree to such an arrangement, knowing they effectively will be acting as banker to their children and have to hope the business will flourish.

Perhaps Chuck and Cathy should hire business planning professionals to help them work out the legal details and binding agreements for the transfer of their business to their family. They no doubt will have to make adjustments to their plan as the situation evolves.

CHARITABLE GIVING

There are a several reasons you might consider including charities as beneficiaries of your estate. For example, you might want to leave behind a memorial to someone important to you or leave a legacy to an organization in whose purpose you strongly believe. Such a bequest would supplement and effectively continue the annual giving you have done during your lifetime. If you have no obvious heirs, your favorite charities may be the logical beneficiaries.

There is a rationale for making both charities and your children beneficiaries, even if your estate is relatively small. Let's say your faith community is very important to you, you have two children, and your inheritance including your home will total $400,000. If your beneficiaries were only your children, each one would inherit $200,000. But what if those children were to inherit only $175,000 apiece? Would they really be materially less well off? If not, you could leave $50,000 altogether to your faith community in addition to the inheritance for your children. This would allow you to both demonstrate, in a practical way, support for your values and, at the same time, your heirs.

If you typically write checks to a number of charities each year, you might consider having fewer charities—those vitally important to you—collect upon your death. You can focus the giving even more by discussing with the charities how your donations will be used and specify that your gifts will support projects of particular interest to you. If your beneficiary charity has its own endowment, you have a choice to leave the money directly to that charity, which might spend it all at once, or to the charity's endowment fund, which will only disperse and spend the interest from your gift each year. The latter alternative means your annual gift will be smaller but will continue benefiting the charity over time.

If you are thinking that the best way to leave money to charity upon your death is to specify that desire in you will, remember that only non-beneficiary assets are processed by your will. A better approach is to direct some of your retirement funds to charity. You do this by making your selected charities the primary or, more likely, the contingent beneficiaries of your retirement plans. You can also direct some portion of your estate to family and the remainder to charity. To do so, you simply fill out a beneficiary form indicating which charities you choose to be beneficiaries; those will collect from your estate only if you had not needed to use the money for yourself.

Because charities do not have to pay taxes on the money they receive, even from retirement plans, whereas your children do, it is more effective to allocate retirement monies to charities and nonretirement funds to family members in your estate plan.

There are other, more indirect ways to leave money to charity. One is to set up a private foundation that you and family members will manage. This is an expensive approach, however, because of the legal and administrative costs, and there are some restrictions on how to manage it. It is worth considering only if the amount to be left is quite substantial. A less costly but somewhat similar approach is to use a donor advised fund (DAF), frequently administered through a large foundation. You make one or more lump-sum contributions and then advise the foundation as to what checks it should write, in what amount, and when. You get the immediate tax deduction when the DAF receives the money, even if it is dispersed over a number of years. Information about DAF funds is private, not public.

What if you could give money to a charity upon your death yet receive a charitable tax deduction now and income for the rest of your life? One way to do this is through a gift annuity, which some larger charities make available to donors. You write a check to the charity for the purchase of the annuity, and the charity then sends you regular checks for the rest of your life. The amount of these payments, which is only partly taxed, is based on current interest rates and your life expectancy. Furthermore, you get an upfront tax deduction for the part of the contribution that will eventually go to charity.

Another approach is to transfer assets, such as cash, securities, or even real estate property or part of a business, to a charitable remainder trust (CRT). This arrangement will provide you an income while you are alive and then transfer the remainder—whatever is left after you are no longer taking the income—to charity. You are also entitled to a charitable deduction during your lifetime, which can be substantial. If the deduction is greater than you are entitled to write off against income in the year of donation to the trust, you can carry forward any unused deductions for up to five additional years.

You can sell any assets inside the CRT without paying any income tax. Only when you take income out of the trust is it taxable. If the CRT is set up appropriately, you can even postpone taking money from it if you do not need to; the trust will then owe you income, which you can withdraw later on. A CRT provides tax deductions and sheltering, while also benefiting your favorite charities. If the CRT is set up to permit it, you can change your charitable beneficiaries.

If you are concerned about disinheriting your children by leaving money to charity via a CRT instead of them, it is possible in some cases to do this by using the tax deduction from the transfer of assets to the CRT to generate payments to another trust holding a life insurance policy with your children as the beneficiaries. This combination of the two trusts can provide income for life, an inheritance for your children, and a major gift to your favorite charities.

If you are interested in charitable planning, work with your financial planner and estate attorney to prepare the required legal agreements.

ANNIE, HER FAMILY, AND COMMUNITY

Annie has inherited all of her late husband Al's IRAs and other investments. Because she has no children, there is no obvious beneficiary for her estate. Her two sisters are financially secure, but her musician brother Doug, to whom she feels especially close, has nothing. Should she leave her money to him but not to her sisters? What about her nieces and nephews?

Annie and Al together helped homeless people as long as they were married, primarily through their professional work. Should she establish a planned-giving/legacy program to support the homeless after she dies? Should she use her will for that purpose? Can she designate it to the memory of her father, Keith, and to Al? Clearly, Annie has charitable intent. She cares deeply about what happens in her community at large and has acted on those concerns for many years. If she feels that strongly, then why wouldn't she want to leave money, perhaps the bulk of her estate, to charity?

For answers to these questions, Annie should talk with planned-giving administrators, the professionals who arrange for legacy gifts at the charity of her choice. Their discussions would include information about long-term visions of the nonprofits Annie supports.

Annie can direct money to charities upon her death by naming them as beneficiaries of her retirement accounts. The recipients will not pay income taxes on retirement money because they are nonprofits, whereas family member would. It will be more appropriate, then, for Annie to direct her nonretirement accounts to family members upon her death since they won't have to pay income taxes on that money when they receive it; she can stipulate that desire by putting on a POD (payable on death) designation onto the nonretirement accounts for that purpose. Assets with a POD avoid probate; using her will for that purpose would subject the assets to probate.

She could even move some nonretirement investments, such as highly appreciated stocks or mutual funds, into a CRT (charitable remainder trust) during her lifetime; those investments would grow tax-deferred in the CRT. Gains would be taxed only when income is paid to her from the CRT. She could take income, as needed, up to a specified percentage, from the trust if is set up to permit such withdrawals. After Annie is finished using the CRT to supply her income, the remainder will go to her favorite charities, either when she wishes or upon her death. Or she can make specific relatives the successor-income beneficiaries, meaning they will receive her share of the income for up to twenty years after her death. Charities would then have to wait an additional twenty years to receive the remainder.

Annie would also receive a substantial charitable deduction for part of the money that goes into the CRT, depending on just how the CRT was set up. She could use that deduction to shelter other income in the year of the donation to the trust and have more money for other purposes.

COMPLICATED ASSETS

When it comes to estate planning, some assets present more complications than others—for instance, those that are difficult to value or divide up, are illiquid, or have multiple owners. These include a vacation home or other property, a business interest, or a partnership. If, say, the cabin you have in a neighboring state is not owned by a trust, it could be subject to probate in both states. Such complicated assets require more detailed planning and frequently more legal documents. Or what if several family members use your cabin? If you make all the decisions about the property yourself, there may not be a problem until you die. After that, however, different inheritors may have different ideas. One may want to sell the cabin and use the money elsewhere, another may want to keep it for herself, and another may want to share the costs and benefits. If one inheritor has the funds to buy the other ones out, the controversy might be resolved that way—or not at all. All by way of saying that there are many details to consider when planning for the outcome of your estate.

GIFTING THROUGH AN ESTATE

Gifts during your lifetime and upon your death are similar in that they are taxed unless they are exempt as described in the last chapter. But there are two important differences.

One difference is that there is what is called "a step-up in basis" upon death. Taxes on any gains or losses up to the time of death are zeroed out unlike gifts during your lifetime.

The other major difference is that you generally give away your IRAs and annuities to your beneficiaries upon your death. If the IRA goes to your spouse and the spouse does not want to cash it out and pay taxes on it, the spouse can take it under his or her own name and postpone paying taxes on it until after the spouse dies.

When those accounts go to anyone other than a spouse, the account is generally cashed out immediately or within five years. When the money is received, taxes are paid on the whole amount by the beneficiary at the beneficiary's rate.

There is still a loophole that can provide an enormous benefit to a recipient who does not need to spend the inheritance right away. It is possible to stretch out payments from the IRA or Roth IRA until the recipient reaches approximately age eighty-five. The money that would have been paid in taxes upon receipt remains in the account and grows through the years. Stretching requires the expertise of an attorney or planner to make sure that it is done properly.

PREPARING FOR YOUR ESTATE

A key question to ask as you begin your estate-planning project is, What are the outcomes I want to avoid? The answers may convince you that doing *something*, even if it is not perfect, is better than doing nothing, risking that a probate court could well make wrong decisions for you. Estate planning may not seem urgent. Yet it is important enough that you should schedule it and get it done before it is too late. Since you don't know when "too late" will be, the time should be now, even before retirement.

Once you have made the critical estate-planning decisions with your spouse or partner, be sure your legal documents accomplish what you want them to.

- Review your life insurance, and consider calling the relevant insurance companies to verify that the policies are still in effect. Do you have some life insurance through work? What additional payments should you make to keep the coverage in effect now and the future?
- Do insurance planning. Is the insurance still cost effective? Annual payments by owners of new life insurance policies have decreased over time as the average life span has increased. Can you substitute a less expensive policy now? Do you have the right kind of insurance—term versus cash policies, single or double coverage policies? Make changes as needed according to your estate plan.
- Review your wills and trusts for possible revisions, and change the instructions according to your current needs and decisions.
- Review your beneficiary designations to make sure they are compatible with your wills and trusts. You should have both primary and contingent beneficiaries for each.
- Make sure that both your durable and healthcare powers of attorney are up to date. After your death, they will be ineffective but can be invaluable before then.

9. If You Don't Have Your Health . . .

The risk of getting sick or becoming disabled is a serious one. Because you may well have a long life, there might be more time for things to go wrong. And naturally, you don't want to spend the bulk of your retirement with doctors.

There is also the fear is of running out of money because of healthcare costs. Healthcare today is much better than it used to be, but it is also more expensive. If you have a partner and either of you gets very sick, you might have enough to pay the costs for the sick one. But will there be enough money left over for the survivor?

The reality may not necessarily be bad, however. You might think that your potentially longer lifespan will include years of sickness and incapacitation. Yet the truth is that, for most older people, sick time and extensive healthcare mostly come toward the end of life. Generally speaking, longer lives mean more years of being functional, with some limitations.

When you have fears about your health, you can choose between fight and flight. Most people take the flight alternative—denying that bad things could happen to them and just hoping for the best.

But you can choose to fight declining health. Perhaps surprisingly, a large proportion of health problems are influenced by choices we make and actions we take. Good choices can make a substantial difference.

HEALTH AND THE QUALITY OF LIFE

To have a high quality of life, you ideally need

- the energy to get around,
- functioning body parts,
- little or no pain,
- your wits, and
- the ability to carry out your physical, social, and emotional responsibilities.

You can live with deficits in some of these areas, but a pileup of health problems makes life more difficult.

CHRONIC HEALTH ISSUES

In 1900, when the average life span of Americans was forty-seven years, the three most common causes of death were pneumonia/flu, tuberculosis, and gastrointestinal infections from contaminated water and other sources.

In the United States today, the four causes accounting for two-thirds of all deaths are heart disease, cancer, stroke, and diabetes. It is not that heart disease, for example, was not a major problem in 1900. In fact, it was worse then. But medical researchers since that time have found ways to combat and even cure some of the acute conditions that killed people at younger ages back then.

Here are some of today's more common chronic conditions:

- cardiovascular conditions, including coronary artery disease, high blood pressure, congestive heart failure, arrhythmias, and stroke

- cancer, formerly acute and typically fatal, but now managed in many cases over a period of years
- diabetes
- bone/joint conditions, including degenerative arthritis of the knees and hips, back pain, and chronic injuries after falls
- kidney disease
- chronic obstructive pulmonary disease (COPD) and other breathing problems
- mental illness, including depression, anxiety, and many others
- chronic or recurring headaches, dizziness, fatigue, and lower-back problems
- sleep problems
- drug/alcohol/tobacco dependency

These chronic conditions can affect both the quantity and quality of your life. On average, having one or two of them shortens a lifetime by a year; three or more shorten life by five years. Yet 75 percent of people age sixty-five and older have at least one chronic condition; 50 percent have two or more.

One chronic health problem can lead to others. Cancer, for example, is not just a disease to be treated and managed; it can have a variety of effects on you and your family such as depression, anxiety, and stress.

YOUR BEHAVIORS AND CHRONIC HEALTH ISSUES

You can make your health situation better or worse. In fact, between 40 and 50 percent of the onset or worsening of chronic conditions are commonly believed to be behaviorally caused or aggravated. Here are some problematic behaviors that can make things worse for you:

- tobacco use. Fewer smokers die from lung cancer and COPD than from heart disease. This is partly because smoking contributes to heart disease, which in turn can lead to heart attacks, strokes, and peripheral vascular disease.

- poor diet. There is no universally accepted view on what makes an optimal diet. Some believe it should contain four equal shares of fruit, vegetables, protein, and grain, with only a small portion of dairy products and little or no red meat. Mixtures of grains, plants, fruits, and nuts provide all of the essential amino acids and are sufficient by themselves to produce complete proteins in the body. A diet rich in sugars and salt and poor in healthy nutrients can lead to obesity and an increased risk of, for example, diabetes, various cancers, heart disease, and possibly dementia.
- lack of activity. This affects obesity, diabetes, and other conditions.
- excessive drug and alcohol use
- exposure to microbial and toxic agents, some of them at your workplace
- excessive anger. Perhaps you've heard of someone dying of a heart attack amid a fit of rage?
- chronic insomnia

Stress plays an interesting role here. If there is not enough of it, you can end up existing without challenges or meaning. But too much stress can be a killer. Long-term stress is different from adrenaline-mediated short-term stress, which enables you react quickly to threat and danger; it is mediated by cortisol from the adrenal gland. When there is too much cortisol present for too long, it can compromise your immune system and lead to problems with healing, clots, plaque, and heart disease.

Researchers have shown that sustained stress is associated with physical problems such as obesity (eating makes you feel better), diabetes, cardiovascular diseases including stroke, Alzheimer's, and elevated fat levels. Excessive long-term stress is also connected to depression, anxiety, fatigue, and Post-Traumatic Stress Disorder.

LESSENING CHRONIC HEALTH PROBLEMS

The development and progression of chronic conditions may seem inevitable. It is entropy in action—the gradual decline into disorder. So how do you combat entropy? By actively using energy to fight it. Having a serious disease can be stressful in itself. Unless efforts are made to reduce the stress, the stress can make the disease worse.

Why not invest time in improving your health? Healthy behaviors are likely, first of all, to prolong the length and quality of your life.

The time you invest may prevent or even delay the onset of chronic conditions. If you already are dealing with one or more such conditions, the time you invest may slow their course or, in some situations, even reverse their development. Here are some avenues that can lead to making a difference.

BECOMING AN EDUCATED CONSUMER

Education will provide the tools you need to make progress in combating chronic health problems. Information may motivate you to gather specifics about actions that can help you change harmful behaviors.

Working closely with your doctor is critical for good health. But you might consider doing more. Many doctors are very conservative in their approaches. They will follow recommendations from the medical establishment, which approves treatments for symptoms and diseases based on a preponderance of evidence that they are effective and safe for most—i.e., they typically do not produce complicated side effects. It can take many years, even decades, for a new medicine to be tested and approved, changes made in recommendations for treatment, and doctors informed and prepared to adjust treatments.

This slow process may be great for the population at large but is not necessarily great for you. When trying to get a health situation under control, you measure time in days, weeks, and months, not in decades. You may want and need to be more aggressive than the medical establishment regarding your own treatment, for example by using drugs approved overseas but not yet approved in the United States.

This can put you in a bind. If you want to take other nonstandard information into account, how do you make decisions about what medicines to take? How much information do you need? What do you do when too much information is out there, especially when some of it is contradictory?

Ultimately, you have to trust. But what constitutes trustworthy, high-quality medical information? Here it helps to understand the process of making medical progress. A key element of medical research is the large-scale, prospective, double-blind study (the researchers and subjects do not know who received the treatment and who did not), conducted with randomly selected subjects. All components of the study—experimental design, selection of subjects, data collection and analysis, and conclusions—are reviewed and challenged by experts in the given field. If the study meets the challenges posed by reviewers, the report gets published in one or another major medical journal.

If the results are particularly timely or pertinent to conditions affecting a great many people, then newspapers, magazines, blogs, and other media will publicize the results. The most rigorous, trustworthy, and best-educated journalists will put the results in context with other studies.

Was the study promoted and paid for by a drug company that ends up promoting its own drug? Is the article you are reading promoting a product or service that the authors will be paid for? If so, that does not mean that the ideas being promoted are wrong. But it at least merits a healthy skepticism. Some drug companies have a history of reporting studies that "prove" their therapies are effective while ignoring or minimizing studies that show their ineffectiveness.

Understanding and acting on medical and health information is part science and part art. The science part involves doing your best to understand the work being done. It includes some understanding of science and math. The math part includes understanding statistical significance and the idea that correlation is not the same as causation. (That is, just because two factors increase or decrease at the same time does not mean that one causes the other.)

Think also about the upside and downside of taking a different approach to treatment. What are the possible best and worst outcomes of healthcare choice A and choice B? But recognize here that our brains are wired to downplay the chances of an unfavorable outcome ("It can't happen to me") and overplay favorable outcomes.

The art part of understanding means connecting different ideas in creative ways. Assuming that the articles you read are not just making things up, is it possible to reconcile articles that appear to disagree? Here are some questions to consider:

- What are the sources of the information being cited?
- How were the studies done?
- Where were the studies published?
- Have you read and discussed the studies with your physician?

So, if you are taking responsibility for your health by being informed means you may end up having better conversations with healthcare providers about options and, perhaps, ways to approach resolving your health issues creatively. If you want to follow a course of treatment that your doctor disagrees with, make sure you understand the risks involved.

Unfortunately, you cannot believe everything you see or hear. Personal testimony is not the same as scientific proof, and is often meant to deceive or sell. Drug advertisements on TV are not particularly helpful. And the Internet is sometimes helpful, sometimes not.

CHANGING HARMFUL BEHAVIORS

Even after you have figured it all out, changing your behavior is a challenge, sometimes even if your life is at stake. Solutions that may be simple are rarely easy in practice. Changes require breaking habits and, sometimes, overcoming physical or emotional dependence.

Many people stop smoking, start an exercise regime, or change their diet and are successful. Others stop bad behaviors or start good ones by working with others through Weight Watchers, Alcoholics Anonymous, treatment centers, or various health professionals.

Here are some harmful behaviors to consider stopping:

- *Stop abusing substances.* People smoke, take recreational drugs, abuse medical subscriptions, and overuse alcohol for many reasons, including mood enhancement and distraction from their life situation. The problems caused are both physical and mental.

  If alcohol is a problem, you will have time in retirement to try tackling it. If you do not make a sincere effort, however, having more time to indulge can make matters worse. But successfully resolving alcohol abuse can markedly improve the quality of your life.

- *Stop letting pain get out of control.* Pain can be debilitating, making it hard to think about anything else. You may not be able to prevent pain from happening, but there are a variety of physical and mental approaches for helping get it under control. Beware of pills such as opioids, which are habit forming. For many, opioids end up being more problematic than the pain itself.

  The physical approaches include acupuncture, massage, and physical therapy. Mental approaches include biofeedback, behavior modification, guided imagery, self-hypnosis, mindfulness, and stress-reduction techniques. Many also believe that medical marijuana can help.

Here are some behaviors that you can consider starting:

- *Start working with your doctor and other healthcare professionals.* This relationship will work best if you approach it as a partnership aimed at improving your health and lifestyle. Like other effective partnerships, it requires time, commitment, trust, listening, respect, and brainstorming on both sides. If not all of these elements are present, find another healthcare provider or a different way of working together.

  In this partnership, you have major responsibilities. One is to educate yourself so that you can have intelligent conversations with your professionals. A second responsibility is to follow the action plan you and the provider have developed and agreed upon, e.g., taking medications as prescribed, exercising, changing your diet, and following up with other healthcare providers.

An effective partnership includes prioritizing in cases where several changes need to be made. Monitor your progress in order to revise the plan as appropriate.

Your doctor's key tools include listening, understanding and educating you, diagnostics, drugs, and surgery. Other healthcare providers may use alternative medical approaches. If the recommendations include changes in your exercise or diet, for instance, you will need to work on them. Your challenge will be to find the personal strength or resources to make necessary changes or to find the right professionals to work with in order to make progress.

SUE AND HER MEDS

Becky has noticed that Sue is taking a large number of medicines. Sue's drugs help control her chronic health problems but may be problematic on their own. When questioned, she says the drugs have been prescribed over the years by a variety of doctors for various ailments. Becky wonders if the drugs might be interacting in ways that could cause harmful side effects.

If Sue does not have centralized medical records from a number of different prescribers, then Becky should bring her and her medicines to her doctor or pharmacist, either of whom can look for drug interactions. The doctor should always be thinking about medications she takes that she could do without.

- *Start getting more and better exercise.* Aerobic exercise—during which you breathe heavily—strengthens the heart and circulatory system by helping you breathe better. Aerobic exercise also burns calories. It reduces the chance of obesity and type 2 diabetes, lowers blood pressure, and improves the immune system. It also can ameliorate stress.

  Strength training provides many of the same benefits as aerobic exercise. It helps with weight control, builds a strong heart, reduces blood pressure, improves cholesterol levels, reduces sugar levels, and improves blood flow. It also increases bone density and improves balance and coordination. You can start strength training at any age to help reverse conditions such as the loss of muscle mass as well as chronic joint and back pain and fatigue.

  Balance and flexibility training exercises help improve mobility and physical stability. Together with strength training, they enable the back, knees, shoulders, and hip muscles to work better.

  Doing these three kinds of exercise could result in your having less pain and fewer surgeries during retirement. It could also result in increased tolerance for other kinds of exercise that will further facilitate quality of life.

  Caveat: If you have even the slightest doubt about your ability to handle any of these kinds of exercise, consult your medical professionals. It may help to meet with a professional, such as a personal trainer, before starting to exercise so that you can learn how to perform the exercises effectively and without hurting yourself. Be aware of the risks of too much exercise—injuries, overuse, and wear on joints. Activities such as yoga, tai chi, bicycling and walking may combine strength, balance, and aerobic benefits with minimal risk.

BRIAN DEALS WITH A CHRONIC HEALTH ISSUE

Brian considers starting an exercise and diet program. Through the years he has gradually put on extra weight but has not been especially concerned about it until now. At his last routine physical exam, his doctor told him he is prediabetic—that is, if he is not careful he will develop diabetes.

Brian should first get a referral from his doctor to the local diabetes education clinic. Then he needs a plan of action. The one he and his doctor develop may include more exercise and a healthier diet. It might be as simple as taking regular walks whose length and pace increase over time, eliminating fast food, and decreasing food and alcohol portion sizes. It also might help him to work with a personal trainer and dietitian. It will take commitment, courage, and time to make progress in this area.

The most important way to get going and keep to his plan will be to have someone to meet with frequently who will provide information, feedback, and encouragement.

- *Start eating healthier food.* Better nutrition, which includes less sodium, sugar, and processed food as well as fewer saturated fats, will help you feel better and reduce disease risk. Take the time to read nutritional labels on processed food. Note that the most abundant ingredients are the first ones listed.

  The so-called Mediterranean diet is frequently mentioned as a healthy alternative. It restricts eating poultry, eggs, cheese, and yogurt to moderate amounts and permits eating red meat only rarely. It also promotes such foods as olive oil, legumes, fresh vegetables, and red wine.

The U.S. Department of Agriculture's dietary guidelines recommend a variety of vegetables, whole fruits, grains (half whole grains), fat-free or low-fat dairy products, and some protein. Less than 10 percent of the diet should be from sugar, and sodium intake is to be limited.

Yes, you need adequate calories to give you energy, but taking in fewer calories can help prevent a slide into obesity. Multivitamins are also helpful, particularly if you do not have a healthy diet.

- *Start sleeping better.* You can invest some of your "extra" time in retirement in getting more sleep. Not only will you feel better, but you will also be more alert. Insufficient sleep is associated with the early onset of Alzheimer's.

  For many people, getting sufficient sleep—six and a half to eight hours per night—can be challenging. Changes that might help in this regard include regular exercise, minimizing caffeine and alcohol consumption, and routine wake-up times. You can consult with specialists in this field for a diagnosis and treatment if adequate sleep is a problem.

- *Start setting up your home properly.* As you age, your balance and reflexes may deteriorate. Most injuries from falling occur in the home. You can set your home up to reduce the chances of this happening. For example, make sure your rugs will not trip you. And you can install railings in the shower and bathroom to steady yourself if the floor is slippery. Install railings on both sides of stairways.

- *Focus on well-being.* There are a number of things you can do to develop a positive attitude aimed at maintaining a sense of well-being as you get older. Developing a sense of gratitude about yourself, your situation, and the world around you can be valuable. Some people even jot down their positive feelings in a journal.

  Being kind and compassionate to others works for some people. Others enjoy being close to nature or to friends and family.

Pausing in your day to focus on breathing and its variations—belly breathing, relaxation exercises, and even prayer—will help you manage stress better.

Connecting with other people regularly can help provide a sense of well-being. Why not start or join a support group—three to eight people who get together to share what is going on in their lives, to listen, to challenge and support each other in their life journeys?

Making these changes can be challenging. Faith and confidence matter.

DOES A HEALTHY LIFESTYLE MATTER?

Developing an orientation around health can be a profound change for most people. Is it worth the effort?

Clearly, good health can mitigate a number of medical conditions. Emerging evidence suggests that it may even have beneficial results for one of the most debilitating and frightening illnesses of our time, Alzheimer's, which affects 10 to 15 percent of older adults. Most people experience some memory loss as they age, but Alzheimer's and other forms of dementia affect up to half of those over age eighty-five.

During the past thirty years, researchers have developed two hundred experimental drugs, none of which has been successful in preventing or curing Alzheimer's or other kinds of dementia. Yet a recent, high-quality, two-year preliminary research study conducted in Finland has indicated that a combination of diet, exercise, cognitive training, and health monitoring/managing helped prevent or delay the onset of Alzheimer's. Other research has shown that poor sleeping habits may increase the incidence of Alzheimer's. (Sleep was not a focus of the Finnish study.)

Study participants ate Mediterranean-style food, took vitamin D supplements, and received nutritional counseling. Their exercise included building muscle strength, balance, Nordic walking, jogging, aqua gym, and calisthenics, and coaching. Cognitive training involved various counseling and computer self-training exercises. Health management included assessments and coaching by physicians and nurses. Unfortunately, since multiple interventions were used at the same, it was impossible to sort out the relative effects of any one factor.

The study was encouraging, but more high-quality data from more participants will need to be collected in coming years in order to ascertain whether this effect is real or not. Will such studies in other countries yield similar findings? Would they work over a longer period than the two years of the Finnish study? Might some other combination of diet and exercise work better? There are a variety of other such studies in the works to help resolve these and related questions.

PREPARING FOR A HEALTHY RETIREMENT

Your health issues can be addressed at any time, and can be part of your preparation for retirement. The first step is to assess your current health, related behaviors, and commitment to improving your health. Then, educate yourself sooner rather than later.

Many times, the solution to a health problem is clear but far from easy. For example, if you are a smoker, the solution is to stop. But that is not easy to do. Approaches include nicotine substitution, habit-reducing medications, and stop-smoking groups. Don't be discouraged if you try and fail. Try again with the same or a different approach. Getting help through coaching is frequently critical.

It is easy to feel out of control when it comes to health problems. Yet if you take responsibility and make the necessary changes, you can improve your health and have a higher-quality retirement.

10. Coming Up with Money for Healthcare

In an oft-performed Jack Benny skit, he is confronted by a robber. The robber asks, "Your money or your life?" Benny takes a trademark long pause, then replies, "I'm thinking, I'm thinking!" It was (and is) funny because who wouldn't pay to save his or her life? But if you are forced to decide between the risk of dying and paying for a drug or a procedure you cannot afford, it is not funny. Yet in this country, that happens all the time.

Healthcare costs in the United States have risen much higher than the rate of inflation for a range of reasons:

- Effective drugs, technologies, diagnostic tools, and treatments are expensive.
- Receiving more effective, continuing care means you may live longer.
- Insurance/payment mechanisms are less efficient than in some other countries, where healthcare typically is better and less expensive than in the United States.
- Many Americans spend substantial amounts on care during the last months of life, often with little health benefit.

Not only is healthcare very expensive, but also its costs are unpredictable. How can you budget for them? If you have a partner, it is bad enough if either of you gets sick and needs costly care. How might that affect future care for the other partner if most of your money has been used up?

TWO HEALTHCARE SYSTEMS

There are two different healthcare systems; you pay for their services separately. The first is for acute health problems. These are problems that are episodic in nature and can reoccur. You pay for them out of pocket or through your health insurance, including Medicare and Medicare supplemental insurance. Acute-care health insurance typically covers all, or a substantial portion of, expenses for physicians and other providers, hospitals and treatments that include diagnostic tools, medicines, and surgery.

The second system deals with chronic health problems, sometimes called long-term-care (LTC)—those that are generally not cured but persist over long periods. LTC includes both custodial care and skilled nursing care. The former provides help with the activities of daily living; the latter includes nurses and therapists. These services are frequently provided by family members or social service agencies in a residential institution or in your home. Seventy percent of Americans need LTC at some point in their lives.

Your best resource for receiving LTC is someone who lives with you, such as a spouse, or lives nearby, such as daughters, daughters-in-law, sons, and other relatives. Friends or neighbors often help out, too.

INSURANCE FOR ACUTE PROBLEMS PRE-MEDICARE

If you work for a large firm, your employer likely provides and pays for some of your health insurance as part of a group plan. Perhaps your partner and dependent children are covered as well. If it is a good-quality plan, most acute healthcare costs are covered, even if those costs are quite substantial.

If your employer does not pick up those costs, yet you want coverage for acute healthcare, you have a few options. One is to purchase an individual health policy retail in the marketplace.

A second option is to use a Health Savings Account (HSA) if it is offered by your employer in place of or in addition to an employer-sponsored plan. The money you contribute to an HSA can be invested and grow. Whatever you do not need for healthcare costs and is leftover when you stop working can be used in retirement. HSAs involve large deductibles yet they lower costs for dealing with serious medical conditions—but not so much when it comes to routine preventive healthcare.

If you have health insurance coverage through your employer and retire or leave work before age sixty-five, when you become eligible for Medicare, you are in what is called the health insurance gap zone. This is where COBRA, HIPAA, or private insurance may come into play. Such plans enable you to continue participating in your former employer's plan for eighteen months through provisions of COBRA—Consolidated Omnibus Budget Reconciliation Act of 1985 (revised in 1999)—as long as you enroll within thirty days of leaving the job.

If your spouse is enrolled in an employer-based plan, you may be able to obtain coverage by switching to that plan as a dependent under the terms of the Health Insurance Portability and Accountability Act of 1966 (HIPAA).

MEDICARE

When you turn sixty-five, you are required to enroll in Medicare, the government program designed to pay some acute-healthcare costs. You can postpone that enrollment if you are still working for a company that has more than a hundred employees and have coverage through it. When you stop working, you have to sign up for Medicare Part B or incur a late enrollment penalty. If your spouse's employer permits it, you can enroll as a dependent in that plan. For questions about Medicare, contact the State Health Insurance Program in your area.

Medicare includes four parts. Medicare A covers hospital costs, Medicare B covers doctors' bills, and the optional Medicare D covers drug expenses. Only Medicare A is free, but the other components of Medicare are generally less expensive than buying policies on your own.

Part B has an income test. Medicare looks at your income for the previous two years as reported on your federal income tax returns. If your income is sufficiently large, Medicare imposes a surcharge on Part B costs.

Because Medicare does not cover absolutely everything and you may have copays for certain expenses, you can purchase a Medigap policy to cover most or all deductible expenses. Or you can purchase health insurance through a Health Maintenance Organization; these offer what is called a Medicare C or Senior Advantage program, which integrates all the types of Medicare and includes Medigap provisions.

LONG-TERM CARE

Medicare does not cover many long-term care (LTC) expenses. If you are discharged from a hospital directly into a nursing home, Medicare will pay for only up to the first sixty days of coverage.

Medicare was originally designed to address acute health problems. Today, if you need care for a chronic condition, Medicare helps pay for hospitals, doctors, and drugs. But it will not cover institutional or home care if you have problems with eating, bathing, dressing, using the toilet, and getting up from and back into a bed or chair. Medicare also does not pay for help with daily-activity problems brought on by dementia.

PLACES TO RECEIVE LONG-TERM CARE

- Your home. It could be family members or professional care providers who come to your home or even live there with you.

- Senior-living facilities. These are also called independent-living facilities or fifty-five-plus housing. Some of them resemble country clubs, with clubhouses, pools, and various activities for residents. Others are basic communities of apartments, condos, townhouses, or single-family homes where seniors live. They do not provide care.

- Senior living with some care. Some of these residences can provide (as extra services) recreation, classes, and common eating areas in addition to private kitchens, and also house-cleaning and laundry. Those may be optional or come as part of the package. Care providers may also be on hand on an intermittent basis.

- Assisted-living facilities. These provide custodial or skilled nursing care but generally on a limited and contracted basis, as part of the package of care services that can be expanded as needs expand.

- Nursing homes. They provide around-the-clock care as needed. If you require full-time attention, these are less expensive than home care.

- Memory care. This includes assisted living or nursing-home care primarily for residents with dementia.

- Respite care. This is for seniors who need intermittent day-time care when their regular provider is not available. Seniors are dropped off at adult daycare facilities.

- Continuing care retirement communities. This is either a single building or a group of buildings where different levels of care are provided. The idea is that you can move from one to another as needed.

If you are about to retire, you will probably not consider any of the above options unless you have an immediate need for care. However, if you are moving out of your home, you could consider independent-living facilities that offer care if and when that time comes.

INSURANCE AND LTC

Buying LTC insurance to cover health risks is hardly your only option. In fact, there are always three possible choices for dealing with such risks, including LTC.

The first is to accept the risk yourself. Sometimes this can work out well. For example, you can enlist a family member's help when you need care. Clearly, this strategy is more problematic if you do not have a live-in partner or nearby son or daughter who is willing and able to provide care. But if you have their support, your situation could get worse, entailing the kind of full-time care that could overwhelm your volunteer provider.

The do-it-yourself option is based in part on the hope that the problem will not arise. But if it does and you have to hire help, the extra healthcare costs involved could seriously deplete your financial resources. In such cases, the person most at risk is your spouse, if all the money for both of you is used to support the sick one.

You can set up an emergency fund to pay for care that may be needed. That fund might need to be quite large. A day of full-time care at an institution costs about the same as a night's stay at a luxury hotel. Full-time home care can cost even more. LTC may be needed for years, particularly to pay for care associated with dementia.

The second option for managing risk is to lessen the risk. Working on improving your health (as addressed in Chapter 9) to prevent or delay serious health problems is a way of doing that.

The third option is to transfer your risk to an entity such as an insurance company by purchasing an LTC policy. This approach has three advantages. First, it can provide a pool of money for paying out-of-the-ordinary medical bills. Second, it can provide tax advantages because some insurance-premium costs are deductible, the amount of the deduction being dependent on your age. Third, it removes some of the uncertainty regarding future treatment costs.

Like most people, you might evaluate this third option primarily in terms of its cost and ask if it is worth it. This is unknowable, of course, because you will only know if it was a good deal, after you have used, or not used, it.

The real role of LTC insurance is to create a predictable cash flow and to protect your assets, just as other kinds of insurance do. When bad things happen and you need the cash, it is there.

You can use a mix of strategies to address the risk of needing long-term care; most people do. For instance, you can buy an LTC insurance policy with a waiting period, frequently ninety days, during which time you self-insure, paying healthcare expenses out-of-pocket. You can also choose a benefit of a few or several years rather than a lifetime of benefits; this is less expensive. Or you can purchase insurance with a more limited benefit that will pay part of the expenses.

If you need LTC–related health services, you will probably prefer to have them available at home rather than at an institution. These days, most LTC insurance policies provide care in either place.

As with other types of insurance, if the bad thing has happened and you now need the care, it is too late to get an LTC insurance policy. But if you are in reasonable health when you apply, you would qualify for the coverage. The older you are, the more likely it is that you will need long-term care coverage in the short run, and therefore will incur more expensive premiums.

HYBRID PRODUCTS

Since the turn of the century, two types of hybrid products—which couple LTC insurance and an annuity or life insurance product—have been developed. These can pay you even if long-term care is never needed. It is much easier to qualify for a hybrid policy than for pure LTC insurance.

The first of these is an annuity, typically a fixed annuity, which includes a long-term-care rider. Not only is the money in the annuity available for LTC for a set a period, typically four to five years, but a second rider can be added to extend benefits well beyond that—even for life. If you do not need the monthly LTC payments for care, you can use the money for other purposes or bequeath it to your beneficiaries. Even if you have a health condition that would disqualify you from getting a typical LTC insurance policy, you can purchase the annuity because you put the money in up front. Even some of the newer variable annuities that provide a guaranteed income for life also have LTC insurance riders. The riders double your monthly income if you are in a nursing home.

The second hybrid product, and currently the most popular one, is a life insurance policy with a LTC provision. The cash value of the policy is available for a combination of future retirement, LTC, and death benefits. Depending on how long you have been paying the policy's premiums, some of the death benefit above and beyond the cash value is available to cover LTC costs.

You can also use the hybrid life insurance approach to opt for a lump sum payment instead of ongoing ones. The death benefit is a multiple of the lump sum, and all of that money can be used to pay LTC benefits. If you do not need long-term care, the death benefit goes tax free to your beneficiaries.

CHUCK'S CONCERNS ABOUT LONG-TERM-CARE

Chuck's father needs long-term-care. Chuck assumed a good deal of responsibility in the family business at a young age because his father Bill, who started The Captain's Table restaurant, had a variety of physical problems, particularly with his back and hips. Bill has been in pain for years and has had multiple surgeries with only moderate success.

Chuck does not know if his father's problems are hereditary, or if the hard labor involved in running the restaurant business brought them on. In either case, he does not want all the responsibility for taking care of Bill, should his father become incapacitated, to fall on Cathy, if Chuck's mother is no longer able to attend to him.

There is nothing like seeing a close family member wrestle with long-term care issues to motivate you to think seriously about this challenge. Chuck is young enough to be able to purchase a hybrid LTC insurance policy over several years and have it all paid up for life. He may be able to buy it through his business in a tax-advantaged way.

MEDICAID

If your income and assets are low enough, you may become eligible for a variation of Medicaid, the federal program that provides medical assistance (welfare) to people unable to afford any, including those who need nursing-home care. This is not a free ride, however. Medicaid has only enough money to pay for the least expensive, and generally the poorest, nursing home services. So, if you are on Medicaid, you may have a lower quality of life than those who are able to purchase health insurance.

Medicaid patients in nursing homes tend to live less long than private-pay patients. Whether this is due to the lower standard of nursing-home care for them or to whatever challenges they faced before entering the nursing home has not been quantified.

PREPARING FOR HEALTHCARE COSTS

When budgeting for retirement, plan to use some of your income to pay for Medicare and its supplements. If you are having trouble evaluating the health insurance alternatives, you can get help from nonprofits that specialize in collecting information on the various options and then reviewing them with seniors so they can make smart decisions. Also, some health insurance agents focus particularly on Medicare.

Many people set aside or designate an asset, such as a certificate of deposit or an annuity, specifically to pay for long-term care if needed. If it is not needed, that asset can become part of the money their beneficiaries will receive.

If this is a route you want to take, you should seriously consider the hybrid LTC insurance option described above. The insurance is as safe as the company offering it, is tax-sheltered, and, best of all, is leveraged. Owning a hybrid LTC policy is a means of protecting assets for a surviving spouse or other beneficiaries after you die. If it turns out you do not need LTC, the death benefit will be paid to your policy's beneficiaries.

You should not delay in taking this approach. In fact, costs increase each year as you age, and if you wait until your health deteriorates, you might not qualify.

PART TWO

What Lets You Sleep at Night: Enough Money

How can you set yourself up so that you do not have to worry about money issues during retirement? The act of retiring feels like an irrevocable decision in an uncertain world. The stakes seem enormous. If you can choose when to retire, you do not want to make a serious mistake by retiring too early. And you may not want to work longer than you have to. You want to get your timing just right.

To be confident that you are set up properly—to be able to sleep at night—you need to address two areas. First, you have to set up your investments so that you get the income you need. Second, you need to ensure that you will be able to make ends meet—in the beginning and throughout your retirement. Living off pensions, Social Security, and investments rather than a regular income from working feels different. Pensions and Social Security may not run out, but investments certainly could.

This section of the book is about how to set up your finances. Doing this right is somewhat complicated but doable. It is worth the effort.

11. Enough Money for What?

Not everyone is fortunate to be able to choose when they retire. The decision might be thrust upon you because of an employment issue—job disappearing, company cutting back, conflicts with a boss—or because of a health issue—your own or that of someone you will be caring for. In these situations, you need your income sooner than you anticipated and must act with more urgency. You have to quickly figure how to get set up your finances for retirement and make decisions about what to do.

If you have some flexibility in your timing, then the word *enough* creeps into the discussion. Do you have enough money to retire now? If not now, then when will you have enough? If possible, you want to address these questions before you pull the trigger and retire. The timing choices you make will depend on many factors, including your resources, family, and health.

If you ask your financial planner "Can I afford to retire?" you might expect a "yes" or "no" answer. However, most professionals equivocate in their answers, perhaps saying "It depends." The follow-up question is "What does it depend on?" How do you get a handle on this question?

ENOUGH INCOME

Before you retire, you are probably focusing on getting by and also on accumulating money to live off during retirement. You choose how much money to spend or save and how to invest it so it will grow. Most likely, your income from your salary is fixed, and making substantial changes to that income and cash flow is not easy.

But during retirement it is the other way around. Your investments are relatively fixed, and you choose how much income to take from them. Your investments, after all, are nothing more than future income. Do you want your income now or later?

When you take income from investments and other sources, you need to match that income against your expenses. This is budgeting. Actually, the question, Do you or will you have enough to retire? is shorthand for, Can you match up your projected income and expenses to have the lifestyle you want? You need a retirement budget to determine whether the match will work throughout your lifetime.

THE TWO TOOLS

To explore what is *enough* for you, you can use two practical and complementary tools: budgeting and projections. Budgeting is short-term and detailed. Projections are more future oriented and big picture.

You can do budgeting on your own with paper and pencil or a computer. You can do projections only through computer programs. Some internet- and computer-savvy people use programs on the internet, but not everyone can do that on their own. Even if you can, the quality of your conclusions will increase substantially if you work with a professional such as a financial planner.

When budgeting and projections are used together, they are powerful. They do more than give you a yes-or-no answer to the question of whether you have enough to retire. They both show you where you stand now and also give you a picture of your finances in the future. They present you with choices you can make about retirement and the possible implications of these decisions.

Confronting the results from these two analytical tools can be painful, particularly if there is a large gap between where you are and where you want to be. Perhaps you realize that your most viable choice to bridge the gap is to continue working. But knowing where you stand, what your choices are, and their implications will benefit you in two important ways:

- The knowledge will empower you. Knowing what will and will not work lets you take responsibility for your actions. You can take a more proactive approach to your finances in your retirement years and feel you have control over what is happening.
- You will experience fewer surprises later—the kind with terrible repercussions. If done properly, budgeting and projecting will give you the perspective needed to successfully prepare for and weather financial storms.

BUDGETING

Budgeting has a terrible reputation, one that may have kept you from having a budget in place in the past. First, people have the misconception that budgeting is difficult and tedious to do. Who has the time and interest to do it when there are so many better things to do? Actually, doing a budget is not as difficult as you may think. It is just matching current expenses with future retirement income.

Second, people mistakenly think a budget is constricting. They believe that having a budget means no longer doing what they want to do. The notion is that you will find yourself saying, We cannot do this because it is not in the budget. But you always have choices to make. The budget may help you better understand your alternatives.

Budgeting can seem scary. What if you do it and discover that you have problems? Do you really want to know about them? Can you accept the results of what you have discovered and act on them? But shining lights into dark places will show you what is really happening and provide ideas for overcoming challenges and difficulties.

BUDGETING MECHANICS

There are two approaches to building a budget. The first, and simpler, is the top-down approach, based on the idea that what you have leftover to spend is the difference between your income and your savings. To estimate what your expenses will be in retirement, look at your take-home pay while working. Next estimate your expenses. If your income and estimates of expenses are right for your current budget, then when you subtract your expenses from your income, the difference is your savings. In other words, income = expenses + savings. If this is not true, then you may have underestimated your expenses. So, adjust expenses up until it is true.

To develop a retirement budget from your current budget, make adjustments that account for what you will be doing differently during retirement, including subtracting your current savings and adding new expenses, for example, for more travel.

The second approach to budgeting is the bottom-up approach. The process has six steps and is more detailed. In this approach, you think through three different alternative lifestyles—Basic, Nice, and Dream. Here is how you do that.

1. *Determine your core expenses first.* From your checkbook or a computer program like Quicken or Money, you determine what you are spending on the main necessities. The categories might be costs for food, shelter (including mortgage, utilities, property taxes, and maintenance), clothing, healthcare, other insurance, transportation, and income taxes. For transportation, you can estimate your annual expenses from maintenance, fuel, insurance, and car replacement costs.

   Be sure to include the cost of replacing your car calculated as an annual payment. For example, if a new car costs $25,000, you keep the car for five years, and you get $5,000 for a trade-in, your net cost would be $20,000, or $4,000 as your annual car payment. By budgeting this cost in, you will not face large "budget-killing" expenses when you replace your car. You can use the funds that you have accumulated to purchase a newer car with cash and save the interest expenses from financing the car.

2. *Determine your Basic Lifestyle.* Add expenses for a minimal lifestyle to the core expenses. These might include costs for recreation such as eating out, entertaining, entertainment, travel, electronics, and others.

3. *Determine your Nice Lifestyle.* Add more expenses to the Basic Lifestyle for a higher level of spending in a variety of areas.

4. *Determine your Dream Lifestyle.* Add still higher expenses to the Nice Lifestyle for a variety of areas. Now you have determined three different possible lifestyles—Basic, Nice, and Dream—based on three different combinations of expenses.

5. *Determine your future income.* List all of your income sources for your current or proposed new lifestyle. If some of your future income will come from investments, assume that investment income will be 3 percent of the value of all of your investments.

6. *Next match your income and expenses.* See how your new income will match each of your different budgets and lifestyles. Tinker with the income sources and your future expenses to explore which lifestyles are feasible.

Does your budget make sense? Which budget—Basic, Nice or Dream—are you currently operating under? At your current spending level, does the difference between your income and expenses equal your current savings or investment withdrawals? If not, you may need to adjust the expenses so that they do match.

What if there is a gap between where you will be and where you want to be? There are two approaches to addressing the issue of having enough. One is to pare back budgeted expenses to match your future income. Can you do this without seriously affecting your lifestyle? Imagine alternatives for each expense. See also Chapter 12.

The other approach is to look for more income from investments or elsewhere. Be sure to include all of your income in your analysis, including Social Security benefits, pensions, part-time work, and investment income. Can your investments work together more efficiently and effectively? Do you need more investments? Would working longer help? See also Chapters 13 and 14.

The creative part of budgeting is assessing your alternative lifestyles and making the trade-offs to achieve the lifestyle you want. Think of your budget as a guideline that provides you with some flexibility. Yes, you can spend somewhat more now because you may be spending less later, especially if you reach an age or circumstance when you do not do as much.

ANNIE'S CASH FLOW AS A WIDOW

Annie, at age seventy, is wondering how Al's death will affect her finances. Will she need to continue working?

Annie's income and expenses will both drop. She will have to live off one Social Security payment instead of two. She will need only one car instead of the two they had. Some expenses, like transportation and medical costs, will decrease.

Annie will use some of her assets to pay for burial costs and estate settlement. But if Al had insurance on his life when he died, then the payout, that is, the death benefit, will be paid to her as the beneficiary and will increase her assets.

At this point Annie does not know how the increases and decreases in income and expenses will play out. If she has not had a budget before, she should make one now. If she has one, she should revise it. In this way Annie can account for the different factors, including retiring or continuing to work, that will affect her future cash flow.

PROJECTIONS

After you have successfully budgeted for your first year of retirement, the next step is to look at what your financial situation is likely to be in subsequent years. You do this through projecting income into the future, taking inflation and possible increased healthcare costs into account. You can use computer programs or work with a professional.

Some sources of future income will increase automatically with inflation, such as Social Security and pensions. Investment income is trickier to include in the mix because investment returns vary so much from year to year. The detailed calculations are complex, but modern computer programs can do those for you.

How much income can you take from your investments without running out before your life is over? You need to estimate future investment returns and their variability for your particular mix of investments, the rate of inflation, your projected life span, and the amount you withdraw each year, adjusted for inflation (see below). When you do this, you can experiment with different estimates to determine your maximum sustainable income with a high likelihood of lasting your entire lifetime.

A large part of the challenge is making good estimates of all of the relevant numbers, but you must also account for the variability of returns from year to year. It matters when the good and bad investment years occur.

Here's why. Terrible returns early in retirement could require you to dip into your savings substantially to draw out the income you need to live on. Such large withdrawals could then shrink your investment pool and limit later income, even causing your income to shrink or run out. On the other hand, good returns early and terrible returns late in retirement are much less of a problem because your money does not need to last as long after the bad times. The unpredictable sequence of returns adds an extra element of uncertainty to your projections.

So, it is not just the returns you receive on investments that count but also when you receive them. Yet you cannot predict when bad things will happen. For your calculations, all you can do is invent a reasonable sequence of returns based on the mix of investments you own and historical returns for that mix, estimate how much money to take from the investments each year consistent with that sequence, and then determine whether you will run out before you die.

The methodology of building a model using different sequences of returns and seeing how the calculation turns out is called Monte Carlo simulations. It is the way projections are done these days. You need to have your computer do the calculations a thousand or even ten thousand times. You can Google *computer Monte Carlo retirement projections* to identify a program that fits your skill level and budget. A reasonable withdrawal rate is one that works for 90 or 95 percent of the calculations for your whole lifetime, thirty or more years.

There are two main uses of Monte Carlo simulations. The first is to provide insight into your future financial situation. You build a model for your investment portfolio and withdrawal rate, and you see how it works. It is those withdrawals that will fund your lifestyle. The second use of the modeling is to derive general guidelines for making decisions about investing.

When you (or your financial planner) build your projection model, here are some things to keep in mind:

- *Returns.* Do not be too aggressive in your assumptions for future returns. If investments are higher priced when you retire than is usual, you should assume somewhat lower returns for the future.
- *Inflation rate.* Bond returns and inflation have been historically low lately. You should consider using a higher, more long-term rate in your calculations, perhaps in the range of 3 to 4 percent, since you should expect that you will be around for a longer time.
- *Life span.* Assume that you will live well into your nineties or beyond. After all, the goal is to have enough, even if you live a long time.

- *Withdrawal rates.* You can experiment with rates between 2 and 5 percent. Anything higher is unrealistic unless you are in your late seventies or older. If you withdraw too much, you will have less money to keep up with inflation.

Don't take the projection results too seriously, down to the nearest dollar. You are projecting way into the future in spite of many uncertainties, which you will be able to understand only after the fact. But here are some of the ways that projections can be helpful to you:

- You can get a sense of the range of results you may achieve based on the decisions you make.
- You can get a better idea of the effects of the risks you take. You will see that investments that are either too safe with low returns or too aggressive with huge variability in results can both be dangerous to your future financial health.
- You can better understand the impact on you of the worst-case scenarios. You should hope for the best but plan for the worst.
- Once you have built the model, you can tinker with it to see the implications of your decisions. For example, you can explore what difference working additional years before retiring would make for your retirement income.

BRIAN'S TIMING OF RETIREMENT

Brian sold commercial products for more than twenty years for the same company before he was recently laid off. He has many questions about how to proceed. At age sixty-four, can he get another sales job? How long would it take him to get established? Does he really want to work that hard? But by far, Brian's biggest question is, Does he have to go back to work? How much difference would it make if he worked another two to three years?

Working longer would increase Brian and Becky's retirement

income. It would accomplish this in three ways.

- First, if Brian is working, they may not need to tap into their savings, and they would have fewer years of retirement to finance.
- Second, if Brian's employer offers a 401(k) or other retirement plan, Brian would be able to add to their investments from his earned income. And if his employer matched some of his contributions, then his retirement savings would grow even larger.
- Third, his investments would have two extra years to grow before he would tap them. Of course, there is no guarantee that his investments would grow. The investments could decrease in value over that time. But on average stock investments do increase in value two out of every three years.

From a financial standpoint, there are two factors to consider when deciding whether to work longer. One is how much greater future income will be if Brian waits a few years to retire. Projections can help answer this question.

The second question is whether that extra income will be meaningful to Brian and Becky. They can answer this question with budgeting. By looking at the different lifestyles and their associated spending levels, they can see what they could do with the extra money.

Since Brian and Becky likely have neither the interests nor skills to do the projection analyses themselves, they would need to get professional help.

PREPARING FOR HAVING ENOUGH

Budgeting and projecting are critical components of preparing for retirement. They will give you insights so that you can make the important decisions about when to retire. It is never too early or too late to do both of these. Earlier is better—you can take control now.

Consider working with a professional for both budgeting and projections. A professional has the skills to nudge you to do your part of the work, has the appropriate computer software for the calculations, and has the experience to put your numbers into perspective.

The analysis you do of budgeting and projections is not a one-time event. As your situation evolves, you will want to review and revise as necessary, perhaps every few years. And doing and learning from budgeting and projecting are both skills that improve with practice.

12. Expenses = Lifestyle

Perhaps you have developed a retirement budget, and you see a potential shortfall. If so, you are concerned that you will not be able to have the lifestyle that is important to you in retirement. So how can you use the budgeting process to make good choices about your life and lifestyle? After all, your budget should not control you—you should control it.

For most retirees, controlling your expenses is easier than controlling income. In fact, there are many reasons you should revisit your future expenses:

- You realize that your expenses are higher than you had originally estimated.
- You are concerned about running out of money because, for example, of changes in your circumstances, the economy, your investments, and so on.
- You are fairly confident that you have enough money, but you would like to have more reserves to take off some of the pressure. If your spending level were lower, then you could use your "extra" money to build up your cash reserves for use on a rainy day.

- Your priorities have changed. You want or need to cut back in some areas of spending so that you have money for the new, higher priorities, whether they are goods or services. The new priorities could be onetime, like your trip of a lifetime, or ongoing, like piano lessons for a grandchild. You know that you can spend your money only once.
- Legacy issues have become more important to you. You would like to spend less money while you are alive so that there will be more of it later for your family or community.
- Your current spending level does not fit who you are. So you want to change your spending so that you can be who you want to be.

CLASSIC APPROACH TO CHANGING EXPENSES

The classic approach to changing your living expenses is to go through them one at a time and look for economies. The obvious categories to evaluate first are your elective expenses. If you need or want to reduce your expenses, then you can reduce your spending on the nonessentials, your noncore expenses.

Reducing your elective expenses may seem straightforward, but those expenses are probably for those fun activities that you are most looking forward to in retirement, such as hobbies and travel. So if you have to cut back your elective spending, don't cut those activities out of your budget. Instead, consider reducing or deferring them or even substituting less expensive activities.

The other category of expenses that you can reduce is the essentials, your core expenses. Here are some ideas for how to do that:

- *Food.* You can prepare more of your food yourself instead of purchasing it in restaurants, coffee shops, and convenience stores. You can experiment with your diet and substitute less expensive food, for example, more vegetables and less meat. If you have the room to store food, you can buy some foods in bulk at lower prices. If you have a serious shortfall, you can use food shelves to supply some of your food.

- *Shelter.* You can downsize to a less expensive place. You can repair small problems before they get big and expensive. If you are renting and have the interest and skills, you can help the owners by, for example, collecting rent from others and doing some of the maintenance in return for lower rent. You can share your living quarters with others, who can contribute part of your costs.
- *Clothing.* When your clothing wears out, you can purchase used clothing instead of new. These days the selection and quality of used clothing can be excellent.
- *Transportation.* You can reduce the number of cars you own and save money on insurance, repairs, and depreciation. If you are doing little driving, you can go car-free and use services like Uber or Lyft when needed. If you continue to own a car, you can keep it longer than you have in the past, until it no longer makes sense, because of mounting repair costs or unreliability. And you can replace your worn-out car with a newer but used car, which will depreciate less.
- *Finances.* Paying bills on time will reduce late fees. Paying off credit card bills each month will eliminate high-interest payments on those cards.
- *Healthcare.* You can reduce costs a variety of ways. Most important are staying healthy through a healthy lifestyle and catching problems before they become untreatable. If you couple these with insurance with larger deductibles or co-pays, you can probably reduce payments over your lifetime.
- *Taxes.* Taxes can be one of your largest expenses during retirement, but lowering them can require making substantial changes to your lifestyle. Moving to a tax-friendlier location, where state income taxes or local property taxes are lower, is one strategy.

  Withholding the right amount of estimated taxes can be a challenge. If you withhold too much, you get a refund after filing but do not have the extra amount available for day-to-day expenses or to add to savings that can generate extra income. If you withhold too little, you have to pay fees and interest on the deficiency.

OTHER APPROACHES TO CUTTING EXPENSES

In addition to reducing elective and core expenses, there are other ways of changing your expenses.

- *Do it yourself.* If you have the time, interest, and skills, you can trade time for money. You can make your lunch instead of going out to buy it. You can make your clothes. You can mow your lawn and wash your car instead of purchasing the services of others.

  You may need to invest in equipment to do these services, for example, food storage equipment, a sewing machine, lawn mower, or car-washing soaps and detailing equipment. However, if you use them enough, they will more than pay for themselves.

  If you make more food, clothing, and so on for yourself than you need, you can barter. You can trade your time or services or things you have made for items or services that you can use. If these are activities that you love to do anyway, then why not do some bartering? You may even get to know your neighbors better.

  There are caveats to consider. You may not have the health to do some activities even if you have the time and interest. And if retirement is at least in part the opportunity to do what you love to do, it makes no sense to do what you hate doing to cut expenses unless absolutely necessary.
- *Buy wholesale.* Your cost per unit decreases if you buy consumer items in bulk. Here the trade-off may be having the space to store items not needed yet. Sometimes you can sign up in advance to purchase many months' worth of items at a discount and even have them delivered over time.

  You may be able to team up with others to buy items in

bulk. For example, you can be part of a CSA (community-supported agriculture) group and buy fresh produce directly from farmers. If your networks are strong and you are creative, you may find many opportunities in the growing "sharing economy."

- *Simplify your lifestyle.* We live in a consumer-oriented society. Marketers and salespeople convince us that we need a large range of goods and services and that we should purchase them right now. Newer is better. As consumers, we expect to get what we want when we want it.

  There is another approach: distinguish between what you want and what you need, and then purchase only what you truly need. Clearly your expenses will be lower if you purchase only what you need.

  A life of simplicity also has a spiritual component. You can focus less on yourself and give more attention to others, perhaps even helping those in need. You can gain huge satisfaction from this different focus on life.

- *Align spending with your values.* If having enough money is a big issue for you, you can look carefully at what you spend your money on. Of course, your spending should be oriented around what is especially important for you.

  You can evaluate if you are too extravagant in some areas of your spending. If so, can you cut back? The converse of this is also important. Are there some areas where you are unnecessarily frugal in your spending? Finding that middle path can be challenging, especially if you have a partner with different ideas about what extravagant and frugal mean.

- *Go with the flow.* If your income changes substantially from year to year, perhaps from changes in total return on your investments, you can always change your spending level. In a year when your income has fallen, you can cut expenses by permanently cutting back on or delaying expenses.

  Be careful, however. If you substantially increase expenses when your income increases, you might break your long-term budget. You need to preserve much of the gain to offset losses in other years.

BECKY CONSIDERS THE IMPLICATIONS OF LIVING ABROAD

Becky studied Spanish in college. After graduating, she had a ball in Spain and has always wanted to go back. Now Brian and Becky are considering spending some serious time, perhaps even retiring, in Mexico, where it is cheaper to live. They might be able to live on Becky's teacher's pension and Social Security when they start collecting. Brian might not have to go back to work. They wonder if this is feasible and if it makes sense for them.

If Becky and Brian want to prepare a budget for living outside of the United States, they should talk with people who have settled in another country so that they can get a realistic sense of what their expenses would be. They need to include possible extensive travel expenditures so that they can visit their family and friends back in the States. The IRS will require extensive tax filing even if they owe no taxes.

The costs to live as expatriates will depend entirely on the kind of lifestyle Brian and Becky want. Costs to buy a comparable place in a desirable location, like Costa Rica or Mexico, may be 15 to 30 percent less than in the United States. The costs to live there would be comparably lower. They would need to consider other issues, like lifestyle, healthcare, safety, and stability.

For some Americans, living outside of the United States has been a last resort to make ends meet. No one knows exactly how many Americans do this, because the U.S. census ignores them, but estimates are that between three and a half and nine million Americans live abroad. Social Security estimates that fewer than 10 percent of them are retirees.

ANNIE DOES NOT LIKE TO WRITE CHECKS

In the six months since Al's death, Annie has taken over the check writing for the family finances. She is finding it to be tedious, and she is losing track of how much money is going where. She could hire a private bookkeeper to help her, but that would be pricey.

Annie can set up her expenses on the computer, but that does not address the tedium of always scrambling to write checks. Another alternative is to have her routine monthly bills paid automatically through automatic bill paying. That would provide three benefits for her: all of those bills would be paid on time, she would have more time for enjoyable and important activities, and nonroutine bills would be more obvious and easier to evaluate as part of her lifestyle expenses.

Even so, she should review her spending occasionally so that she has more understanding and control over her overall finances.

PREPARING FOR MANAGING EXPENSES IN RETIREMENT

Budgets are particularly important in helping you make decisions about your future life. As you think about your many alternatives, your budget will be a powerful tool for understanding the monetary components of your choices.

A written budget can clarify your thinking. You can easily pick up your previous analysis from where you left off and explore other alternatives.

If you are stuck on how to cut expenses, you can break your expenses down in more detail and then look at them. If you are using an expense-tracking program like Quicken or Money, you can easily generate reports with more detail for your review if you want them.

13. Investment Income

Income from your investments may comprise a significant part of your retirement income. Following are the three most likely questions that you may have about retirement income from your investments:

1. How much income can you safely take from your investments?
2. Which types of investment accounts should you take your money from first?
3. Which stocks or bonds should you cash in first?

THREE APPROACHES FOR PREDICTABLE INCOME
When you are working, you probably take for granted two important features of your income: it is predictable, particularly if you work for someone else, and reliable. Most people want a similar experience when they are retired.

There are three independent approaches to generating predictable income during retirement. Each has its advantages and disadvantages. You do not have to choose one of them for yourself. Many people use a combination of all three. If so, you will receive multiple checks from multiple income sources and accounts, which is different from your preretirement days, when your primary source of income may have been only your paychecks.

The first approach is to put your money in *investments that are themselves predictable*. Here are some examples listed in increasing order of risk:

- bank accounts and money market funds
- bank certificates of deposit, which have a guaranteed payout over time, typically from a few months to several years
- bonds of all kinds, which have a regular payout over the lifetime of the bonds, a few years or in some cases as long as fifty years

This alternative can be the safest of the three, although the investments have relatively low returns. They should be part of your portfolio. However, you will need many, many millions of dollars of investments to provide sufficient retirement income if this is the only alternative you use. And then you will use up much of your money because your returns will not keep up with inflation.

These investments are only as safe as the entity making the guarantees. When you own them, you are relying on the credit worthiness of the company or government issuing them. If you find bonds with exceptionally high returns, they will probably have exceptionally high risks for either the payout or the return of your original investment. Of course, bank accounts are insured by FDIC, a U.S. government agency.

The second approach is to invest in *guaranteed contracts (annuities) from an insurance company*. These investments, called immediate annuities, pay more than the alternatives above because they pay you both interest and some of your principal investment on a regular basis. Actuaries from insurance companies review mortality tables to calculate how much to pay you for the return of your principal when the income will stretch over a lifetime.

You can choose to have the guaranteed income last as long as the joint lifetime for you and a partner. When you select a lifetime benefit and then die young, no money is leftover for beneficiaries.

Alternatively, you can receive a slightly smaller income but have a guarantee of some minimum number of payments, so some money would be left for heirs if you died soon after starting to receive payments.

So why not just purchase an immediate annuity upon retirement and be done with your investment planning? The problem with this approach is that you have converted an asset to an inflexible stream of income. You no longer have access to your investment if you need it, and some of your expenses may not be so regular.

Over time your situation can change substantially. Your health and energy level could change so that your activities and the associated expenses are different. Or your family structure could change. For example, your parents or children could require more or less help and support. Your concerns and activities are likely to evolve and change. Your expenses for travel or gifting or care, for example, could radically increase or decrease, depending on a variety of circumstances.

In recent years insurance companies have developed a variation of annuities that addresses their inflexibility. You can purchase a deferred annuity with a rider (option) that provides you not only a guaranteed income but also access to any of the money in the annuity. If you withdraw more than the guaranteed income amount, some of the guarantees for future income decrease. If you die at a young age, money may be left over for the inheritors of your estate.

As with any investment product with guarantees, that guarantee is only as strong as the company issuing it. However, many insurance companies have weathered the Great Depression and other economic difficulties over the past 150 years.

ANNIE SQUEEZES INCOME FROM HER INVESTMENTS WITH GUARANTEED ANNUITIES

Because Annie is interested in having some of her money go to charities for causes that are important to her, she is considering mentally splitting her money into two parts. One part she would leave to chari-

ties, perhaps upon her death, and
the other part she would live on. She
wants to squeeze every nickel of income out of the second part for herself. Is this feasible and desirable?

Such an approach is feasible and
actually easy to accomplish. Annie
could research immediate annuities
from several life insurance companies to determine which would
have the largest payout for her. The annuity would pay her interest
and principal over her lifetime, no matter how long she lived. She
could choose to take a little smaller payment and have her charities
collect the payments if she died within the first five or ten years.

However, this approach would not necessarily be desirable. Annie
would have no cushion if she needed money for healthcare, gifting,
or a new car, unless she had additional funds designated for those
purposes. If, however, she is happy having the charities inherit after
she is finished using her money, a variety of approaches are available to her instead. These include having charities as beneficiaries of
her retirement plans or will, or even setting up a charitable trust (see
chapter 8).

The third approach for predictable income is *mechanical*. You arrange to have some of your income sent to you regularly from your
investment accounts, possibly even deposited directly into your
checking account, like your paycheck was, no matter what the recent
returns on your investment have been. When you run out of cash in
your account, you just cash in an investment to replace used-up cash.
This process makes your investment income predictable and regular.

This is the most common approach because you can use it for any
investment portfolio, even if it contains unpredictable investments
like stocks. When you own stocks, much of your return is dependent on the growth of the companies that you own, in addition to

any dividends you receive. So you cash in some of that growth and live off that over your lifetime.

THE 4 PERCENT RULE

A mechanical strategy offers the possibility of higher returns that keep up with inflation and provide a nicer lifestyle. It requires that you set up your investments properly and take income out in an efficient way.

Determining the maximum sustainable income that you can distribute from investments containing stocks is hugely important. Retirement planning researchers have spent the past couple of decades estimating how much income you can take. What is the magic number?

Researchers used Monte Carlo modeling to answer this question. They assumed that the investor has an investment portfolio comprised of both stocks and bonds of differing mixes, but frequently 60 percent stocks and 40 percent bonds and cash. They used historical investment returns and inflation rates in their calculations. They then calculated the probability of the investments lasting for differing amounts of time, typically from fifteen to forty years.

The researchers concluded that for a withdrawal rate of 4 percent or less per year, there was a 95 percent probability that the income would not run out over a thirty-year period. So if you take out more than 4 percent in the early part of the thirty years, then either you have to take out less later on or run out of money sooner.

Let's look at an example of how the 4 percent rule works. Assume that your retirement budget is for a $60,000 lifestyle in the first year of retirement and that your spending will increase each subsequent year to keep up with inflation. Assume that your Social Security benefits total $35,000 in the first year and that your investments total $500,000. The 4 percent rule says that you could comfortably take 4 percent of $500,000—$20,000—from investments in the first year. If inflation over the following year was 2.5 percent, then you would withdraw $20,000 plus another $500 (2.5 percent of $20,000) for inflation, whether your investments increased or decreased in value over the year.

Note that the sum of Social Security and investment income in this case would be $55,000 in the first year. If your desired lifestyle incurs $60,000 in expenses, then you will have to make tough choices.

CAUTIONS ABOUT THE 4 PERCENT RULE

If only it were true. The 4 percent rule has been popular because it is easy to apply to any situation. But is it right, is it prudent to use it? Possibly not. Here are some of the caveats for applying it in the future.

- For the 4 percent number to work in the future, future average stock and bond returns and the inflation rate would need to be similar to past numbers, since the research is based on data from 1926 to 2016. But the stock and bond returns and inflation rates in the past couple years have been substantially different.

  Are the long-term numbers the best guess? Or are more recent numbers the "new normal" and more predictive of the future? Where the long-term numbers will be in the future is anyone's guess.

- Future stock returns are somewhat predictable based on their relative price, that is, how cheap or expensive they are now. The measure of relative price is the price-to-earnings (PE) ratio, which is how much you need to pay for $1 of earnings. Valuations of stocks go through cycles. If you purchase or own stock when their relative prices are abnormally low, then the returns over the next decade are frequently unusually high. If stock prices are abnormally high, then the returns over the next decade are frequently unusually low. This is because of a tendency for PE ratios to return to historic levels, which is called reversion to the mean. Clearly, to start taking your 4 percent withdrawals when the PE ratio is high is riskier. Right now, stock prices are slightly more expensive than usual. The implications for future withdrawal rates remain to be seen.

- Monte Carlo modeling has been done for different stock and bond mixes. The sweet spot for the mix is between 30 percent and 70 percent in stocks. That is a wide range. If you have less stock than that, it is unlikely that you will be able to withdraw 4 percent sustainably with increases for inflation. You will not have enough returns to accomplish that. If your portfolio is nearly all stock, then going through bad economic times, particularly in the earlier part of your retirement, will damage your portfolio enough that the chances of sustainability will be substantially reduced.

- Is the 4 percent rule a law or a guideline? If it were a law, then it would apply everywhere all the time. In fact, this rule does not seem to apply to sustainable withdrawal rates in other countries.

REMEDIES FOR CAUTIONS ABOUT THE 4 PERCENT RULE

You can make modifications to the 4 percent rule that can increase the chances of your having sustainable income throughout your lifetime.

- *The higher-reserve method.* Reduce the portfolio withdrawal rate during retirement from 4 percent to 3.5 percent, 3 percent, or even 2.5 percent. Taking out less money initially establishes a higher reserve to tide you over during difficult times. This approach would definitely increase the number of years that your future income is sustainable.

  But using this approach has a cost: you will have a less expensive lifestyle in order to make ends meet. If the worst economic scenarios do not happen, then you may die with a substantially larger inheritance than you wanted or needed. This is a good or bad outcome, depending on how much sacrifice you had to make and on how important leaving a larger legacy for your family or community is to you.

- *The slowing-down method.* Start with a 4 to 5 percent withdrawal amount, but plan to decrease your spending as you age. The rationale is that you will have more energy, better health, and a bigger backlog of things to do earlier in retirement than later on. Perhaps you implement this by not increasing investment distributions from year to year, even though costs go up. This would be one form of cutting back.

- *The guaranteed-income method.* Use some annuities to supplement regular income from Social Security and pensions. Having this source of regular and guaranteed income will make you less dependent on the periodic growth of stocks, particularly in those times when stock prices fall. This will increase sustainability.

- *The nontraded method.* Invest some of your portfolio in less liquid securities, for example, certificates of deposit instead of bank accounts, and nontraded REITs or private equity stocks instead of the publicly traded versions of the same investments. On average those investments will have slightly higher returns and possibly less volatility.

- *The cut-back-response method.* Couple your income at least partly with the performance of your investments. So, for example, if your investments have fallen in value over a year because you have spent more money than you have earned from them, then forgo the inflation increase to the investment income during the next year. A more extreme but more effective approach is to cut back on investment income in those years when investments fall in value. You can do this by postponing some elective expenses and activities until investments have recovered from their declines. For example, you can wait to take a big trip.

- *The wait-it-out method.* Use a sell-high approach to harvest investment income. The strategy is to keep enough cash available in some of your investment accounts so that you can ride out any large fall in the market. One to three years' worth of income from investments should be sufficient. You periodically replace used-up cash by selling stocks and other investments as needed.

Here is how this method works. Your regular income is paid out to you from your cash. Then, you regularly, perhaps once or twice a year, decide whether to replace the used-up cash. You establish rules for the decision so that you take the emotion out of the process. For example, you replace the cash if your stock investments have increased by a certain percentage. If not, you do not replace. The details of the rules should depend on your tolerance of risk. Living by the rules will do less damage to your investments because you will avoid selling at low prices. This will make your income more sustainable.

You can combine these methods with each other. Each is more complicated and takes more time and work than using the 4 percent rule by itself. But they may permit you to get more horsepower from your investments and to lead a more meaningful life.

PRIORITIZING ACCOUNTS FOR WITHDRAWALS

Now that you have guidance about how much money you can take out of your investment portfolio, you have to decide which pool of investments—IRAs and other retirement accounts, Roth IRAs, personally owned accounts—you should withdraw money from first. This question has a tax-driven answer.

The main principle is the same as when you are saving money for retirement: postpone paying taxes as long as you can. Money that you pay in taxes is no longer available to continue to grow in your accounts.

In general, you want to cash in nonretirement accounts first. If those accounts contain stocks or other investments with capital gains, you may want to sell those last—after selling investments with little if any gains—again to postpone paying taxes. If your investment mix changes because you sold bonds or other nonstock investments first and now have too high a proportion of stocks in your whole portfolio, then you can rebalance your portfolio by making changes inside your retirement accounts. Making changes inside retirement accounts does not generate taxes.

Your second line of defense against taxes, after you have used up your nonretirement accounts, is to use your Roth IRAs for income. See Chapter 17 for a discussion of Roth IRAs. Withdrawals of the initial investment amount from Roth IRAs are not taxed and neither is any investment income as long as you have had any Roth IRA for at least five years.

Using retirement plans or IRAs to fund your retirement is expensive. Because withdrawals from those accounts are taxed the same as earned income, you need to withdraw $150 to have $100 to spend if you are in the 33 percent tax bracket (federal plus state). This contrasts with taking money from a personally owned bank account, where a $100 withdrawal gives you $100 to spend.

PRIORITIZING INVESTMENTS FOR SALE

Both your retirement and nonretirement accounts may have a mix of stocks, bonds, cash, real estate, and other alternatives. When you need to sell investments to free up cash to distribute as income to yourself, if you have a choice, which kind of investments should you sell first? Consider three choices: stocks first, bonds first, or stocks and bonds in proportion to their amount. Here are the arguments.

Selling stocks first will result in your portfolio having fewer and fewer stocks, resulting in more conservative portfolio—you will be taking fewer risks in the future. This approach will also make your portfolio less growth-oriented and could limit potential return over your lifetime. Selling bonds first will result in the opposite: more growth and more risk over time.

Researchers have compared these two approaches, called *glide paths*, which are gradual drifts one way or the other. They used historical returns, but the same average returns over thirty years, to do Monte Carlo modeling. The differences between approaches were small but statistically significant. The highest returns and the most lifetime income resulted from starting out conservatively and gradually investing more for growth as you age! The explanation given was that your biggest financial risks in retirement are in the beginning. If your portfolio is damaged from substantial falls in stock values early on, that will increase your chances of running out of money sooner. But if you need the returns from growth investments like stocks, you can add them gradually to your portfolio.

Selling stocks and bonds in proportion to the amount of them in your portfolio is tantamount to keeping the same mix of stocks and bonds throughout your retirement. Your investment performance will then be between the upward-sloping and downward-sloping glide paths.

There is another approach you can use: the *wait-it-out harvesting method*, a variation of the wait-it-out method described above that manages risk over your lifetime. This method will not only add slightly to returns but will also lessen the discouragement you might feel when stocks decline substantially, which is almost certain to happen sometime over a thirty-year retirement. Here is how the harvesting method works.

For each account from which you will be needing cash, you start by selling some securities so that it has a pool of cash in it. For example, perhaps after taking Social Security and pension income, you need only an additional $20,000 annually in cash from your IRA. Then your cash pool might total $60,000, enough for three years of distributions. Once every six to twelve months after you have made your distributions and partially depleted your cash pool, you decide if and how you are going to replace the cash.

If stocks have increased in value substantially over that time, then you harvest some of those gains by selling stock and replacing the depleted cash. If stocks have decreased in value substantially, you either defer replacing the cash for a while or you sell nonstock assets to replace the cash. By using this process, you avoid "selling low," and you rebalance your portfolio at the same time.

PREPARING FOR RETIREMENT INCOME

Here are some of the key steps to take to prepare for taking retirement income from your investments.

- *Set up a checklist to catalog all income sources that you receive.* During retirement, you may receive income from a variety of sources, more than you had when working. Keeping track will alert you if anything gets lost in the mail. It will make income tax filing more straightforward, and the checklist can also serve as a base for periodically reviewing your income and expenses to make sure that you are on track.

- *Diversify your portfolio.* You can do this to some extent at any time. It becomes more feasible, however, when you transfer your 401(k) and other retirement plans currently at work to your IRAs and determine your investment mix. Then you have a full range of investments to choose from.

   Effective diversification is particularly important during retirement (see Chapter 16). Your investment mix determines the magnitude of fluctuation in your portfolio values. You can choose the risk level that you are most comfortable with. Diversification will lessen the fluctuations in the value of your portfolio, at least somewhat. The stabler your investments are, the easier it will be to take a steady income from them.

- *Consider including annuities in your investment portfolio.* You can extend your income distributions over a lifetime for yourself and your partner, even in the worst case where you use up much of your investments because you or your investments do not behave as planned. If you outlive your investments, Social Security, pension, and lifetime annuity income will be all that you have to live off.

- *Set up cash pools in accounts from which money will be taken.* You can set these up anytime, but if you have a choice, doing so gradually after stocks have risen in value one to five years before you will need the income may work better. Once you have set up the cash pools, you can continue to harvest gains from rising stock values.

- *Plan your process for making distributions.* Multiple approaches for taking cash income from your investments are available, such as the 4 percent rule and other methods described above. Each will have implications on your future lifestyle. You can use budgeting and projections and integrate them with the income distribution choices you make so that you end up with a feasible and desirable lifestyle.

- *Write up your process in an Investment Policy Statement* (see Chapter 18). Having a written plan will hold you accountable for your future actions and let you have more control over the financial and nonfinancial life that you want to lead.

14. Income from Other Sources

You may well have other sources of retirement income in addition to distributions from your investment savings. Here are the six most common sources:

1. your government pension in the form of Social Security
2. any employee pensions that you have accrued from previous jobs
3. part-time work
4. royalties
5. proceeds from the sale of something valuable
6. largesse (gifts) from family and friends, including inheritance

SOCIAL SECURITY: ITS IMPORTANCE

Thinking through your Social Security options is important for two main reasons. The first is that the amount that you and your partner will collect over your lifetimes can total as much as one or two million dollars if you have been a higher wage earner and you live a long time. Even if you have accumulated substantial savings, Social

Security payments can still account for a third of your retirement income. If you have not been a successful saver, it will constitute the lion's share of your retirement income.

Second, in contrast to ten years ago, we better understand the strategies that you can use to maximize your payments. Claiming your benefits in more effective ways has become important.

In the old days (pre-2005) collecting Social Security was simple. You stopped working and collecting your paycheck, and started collecting Social Security checks. The majority of people still set up Social Security that way.

More recently people have realized that they do not have to couple retirement with collecting Social Security. If you are working, you can collect Social Security, or not. And the same is true if you are retired—you can collect Social Security, or not. In any case, you can still start to collect as early as age sixty-two (sixty if you are widowed) or as late as seventy. Every month you wait to start collecting after age sixty-two the benefit increases, until it maxes out at age seventy. The monthly benefit nearly doubles if you wait to collect at age seventy as compared to age sixty-two. Be aware, however, that if you earn money before your full retirement age (see below), your benefits will be reduced for those years before your Full Retirement Age (FRA).

Perhaps you feel like you have earned this government pension. After all, you have paid into the system for decades, and now you will be getting your own money back. Actually, that is not how it works. There is no pool of money out there with your name on it that you will be cashing in someday. Each year, workers pay into the system, and retirees receive money from it. Your total lifetime benefit can be far less than you paid in if you die young, whether you are wealthy or not. Or it can be far more than you have paid in if you live a long time, whether you are poor or not.

Social Security is an IOU from the government to you and others who have contributed to it. If more money goes into the system than is paid out during the year, the excess becomes part of the Social Security Trust Fund, which has accumulated a trillion plus dollars owed for future payments. If over time the trust fund were to be liquidated and more money is to be paid out than is being paid in, then the government would have to reduce payments from then on. Based on the demographics of baby boomers, that could occur around 2033 if Congress takes no action. The amount of the reduction is estimated to be 25 percent.

Social Security cannot collapse entirely, because there will always be people paying in, and those payments will be made to recipients at that time. But to continue current payout levels, Congress needs to find a way for more money to go into the trust fund, perhaps by increasing the rate contributed by workers or employers, or by distributing less money by, for example, increasing the age one can collect.

SOCIAL SECURITY: ITS FEATURES

Lifetime benefit. Unlike your investments, Social Security pays you from the time you file until you die. Those payments are guaranteed; they will not run out. The longer you live, the more you receive. The program was designed to prevent poverty for the elderly, and it works well at achieving that objective.

Full retirement age (FRA). This is the age at which you collect your full retirement benefit. For those born before 1955, your FRA is sixty-six. If you were born in 1960 or later, then your FRA is sixty-seven. Intermediate birth years have intermediate FRAs.

Amount of benefit. You need to have worked for at least forty quarters—ten years—to be eligible. Two factors determine the amount of your benefit. One is your age when you start to collect, and the other is your average income over your thirty-five highest, but not necessarily consecutive, years of earnings, adjusted for inflation. If you have not paid into the system for all of the thirty-five years, then they will put zeros into the calculation of your benefit.

Do you know what your monthly benefit will be? The Social Security form you receive shows you up to three different amounts for the monthly benefit depending on the age you start to collect: at sixty-two or your current age whichever is higher, at your FRA, and at age seventy. You can also set up an account at www.ssa.gov to see the numbers.

Inflation adjustment. In most years an annual inflation adjustment increases your benefit for that and all subsequent years.

Spousal coverage. If you are or have previously been married (widowed or married for ten years and divorced), then you may be eligible for either your own or a spousal benefit. Your spousal benefit is up to half of your spouse's benefit at their FRA. To be eligible to collect, your spouse must already be collecting, unless you are divorced or widowed. You can collect only one benefit—your own or a spouse's—at a time, although you can switch from one to the other if the new benefit is higher.

Survivor benefit. If you and a spouse or ex-spouse are both collecting and one of you dies, the survivor automatically gets the higher of your two benefits.

SOCIAL SECURITY: STRATEGIES TO CONSIDER

If you are a never-married individual, the only decision is when to start taking your benefits. If you are currently or formerly married, you can use several different claiming strategies that involve spousal benefits and sometimes switching between your own and spousal benefits. Some strategies work a lot better than others.

Wait to collect. If possible, postpone filing until you are seventy unless you are single and in poor health. The longer you wait before filing for your benefit, the higher your benefit will be. Of course, waiting means that you are passing up the benefit before filing. So how long do you have to live to make it worthwhile to wait? If either of you lives beyond age seventy-nine, which is quite likely, it pays to wait.

Maximize the higher benefit for couples. The higher wage earner should wait as long as possible, up to age seventy, before starting to collect. The waiting will affect the benefit not just of the higher wage earner but possibly of the surviving spouse as well.

Coordinate working and filing. Before your FRA, your monthly payments will be reduced if you earn more than the threshold amount, so it is not to your advantage to file for benefits before your FRA if you are still working.

Consider working while collecting. If you are working and collecting at the same time, that is, after your FRA, Social Security will annually recalculate your benefit to replace lower numbers with higher ones and increase the benefit accordingly. So if you or a spouse have been out of the workforce for a number of years, working at older years can be a way to make up for lost work time.

Coordinate Social Security and investment income. Because the benefit increases by 8 percent per year after your FRA, it may pay to wait to file. If you have stopped working, you will still need an income to live off. So while you are waiting to file, you may need to dip into your investments to tide you over.

Do your research. Social Security staff can determine exactly what your own and your spousal benefits, if appropriate, are and which is greater. They cannot advise you about planning strategies for married couples. Consider using a computer program or a professional with experience to evaluate the alternatives available to you. A more effective strategy could net you tens of thousands of extra dollars over your lifetime.

PENSIONS AND OTHER COMPANY PLANS

You or your employer or both of you may have been putting money aside for your eventual retirement. The most common approach is the company retirement savings plan, of which there are two types: defined contribution (a pool of investments) and defined benefit (a stream of income).

DOUG HUNTS FOR PENSION INCOME

Doug at age fifty-six has had inter-mittent jobs as a performing artist, and he doesn't think a lot about money. Even so, he wants to know what income he might have for re-tirement. He has heard through the grapevine that he may have some kind of pension from the or-chestra when he retires, but he has never checked it out.

Doug can easily contact the benefits professional in the orchestra's human resources department. Any of Doug's past employers may have had retirement plans that he might have participated in. When Doug puts together budgets for retirement, he should contact them to see if money will be waiting for him then or when he is older.

Defined contribution plans. These are retirement plans to which you, as an employee, or your employer contribute regularly. They are now the most common form of retirement plans and include a 401(k); its equivalent for employees of nonprofits, called a 403(b); a Simplified Employee Pension (SEP); a SIMPLE IRA; a 457 plan; and others. You have a few choices about what to do with the money or investments in the plan once you have left your company:

- The first choice is to leave it with the company. Many employers discourage this because they do not want to continue to pay fees for administering your account. Managing the account, that is, taking periodic distributions during your retirement, is also cumbersome for you. The complexity of investment management is compounded if you have multiple corporate retirement accounts from different employers and then need to schedule distributions for your income.

- Your second choice is to cash in your retirement plan, but such a move will subject the whole amount to income taxes unless you roll your money over to another retirement plan or Individual Retirement Account (IRA) within sixty days. You are permitted to make only one such rollover every twelve months.

- The third option, which is the most common and frequently the best choice, is to do a direct transfer of your retirement plan into an IRA you have already set up. In this process, sometimes called a 1035 exchange, your money at one institution goes directly to another institution without your cashing the check. There is no limit on the number of these transfers that you can do in a year. Once the money is in your IRA, you have control over its investment and disbursements as you need them.

Each of these direct transfers, or rollovers, is listed on the 1099 tax form sent to you and the IRS, and you must report it when you file taxes. But you do not pay taxes on the amount transferred in this way.

Defined benefit plans. These are employee pensions that provide a direct income to you upon your retirement. They used to be common but are not anymore, unless you are an employee of one of a few large corporations, a union member, or a government employee, such as a teacher. A plan like this will generally pay you a lifetime of income based on your recent highest income and the number of years of service. The plan may have an inflation provision that increases the amount paid out annually based on increases in the Consumer Price Index, the government's calculation of inflation.

Many pensions require that you work for a number of years before you become eligible to receive one when you retire, that is, when you become vested. For example, the pension plan could require that you meet the rule of ninety: you are vested when the number of years you have worked plus your age equal or exceed ninety. So if you started work at age thirty, for example, and you are now sixty, then you have worked there for thirty years, and you are eligible. Or if you started at age forty and you are now sixty-five, then you have worked there for twenty-five years, and you are also eligible.

If you have such a plan, then you have two key decisions to make: when to start the payouts, and whether to include a partner in the payout.

When should you start to collect? Pensions like these typically have three time ranges to consider. You should review the numbers carefully before you make life-changing decisions.

1. The time before vesting, when you are not yet eligible to receive it.
2. The years when you are vested and your benefit increases substantially from year to year. Your employer may have such a provision to encourage you to work to a certain age. It could be worth your while to continue to work for another year or more just to get vested and then achieve a progressively larger benefit.
3. The years when your benefit increases only slightly each year. An employer may have such a provision to encourage you to leave and make room for younger employees. At this stage it might not pay to continue working unless your salary is substantially greater than the pension payout. You might be paid the same amount whether you work or not. You could, in theory, collect your pension, work somewhere else, and collect both incomes.

Should you include a partner as a beneficiary if you die first? Generally, you want a surviving partner to receive at least some if not all of your pension income. You can accomplish this in two ways.

One is to have the pension distributions paid out over both of your lifetimes, although you will receive a smaller monthly benefit than if it were paid over just your single lifetime. The second is to collect only over your lifetime and use some of the money you receive to purchase a life insurance policy. If you die first, the death benefit can provide a monthly lifetime of income to your partner. This approach is sometimes called pension maximization. You should determine which alternative will work better for you.

If you have an employer pension, look carefully at its provisions. Some have a "spring-back provision." If you opt for the spousal inclusion provision, that is, take the distribution over both lifetimes, the benefit is lower than it would be over just your life. If your partner dies before you, some pensions increase the amount paid to what it would have been without including your partner. This spring-back provision is particularly beneficial to you because you are paying for the extra coverage only when you need to.

Combination plans. Some company retirement plans give you a choice between a stream of income and a lump sum payout when you retire. Look carefully at the deal. If you are seriously considering the stream of income approach, then you should compare the payouts with those from a commercial annuity, which you could purchase with the lump sum. You would do this through a 1035 exchange, that is, a direct transfer from the retirement plan into an IRA annuity, which would pay income and principal to you over your lifetime.

Stock purchase plan. In this alternative your employer permits you to buy company stock at a discount inside your retirement plan. If the stock has appreciated, you have two ways to take a distribution of the stock.

One is to postpone taxes by transferring the stock along with your other investments into your IRA. Once there, you could sell it, perhaps to diversify your investments if your company stock comprises a large part of your portfolio. All of the money, including the purchase price of the company stock, will be taxed at your regular tax rate, but only when it is distributed to you from your IRA as income.

The other approach also permits you to postpone paying taxes, but you cannot sell the stock. It is a two-step process. First, you transfer all of the noncompany investments to your IRA. Then you transfer the company stock to a separate account. If this is done properly, the company stock is not taxed until it is sold. Any gain above the original purchase price is called net unrealized appreciation (NUA). When you sell the company stock to generate some income, you pay taxes only on the NUA at the lower capital gains tax rate.

Options to purchase company stock. If you have received stock options that are vested and unexpired, you are generally required to exercise them upon your retirement. Such options permit, but do not require, you to buy company stock at a particular price before they expire. If you cash out the company stock you receive from the exercise of the options, you can use the proceeds as income. Be careful about the choices you make. The tax rules are complicated partly because there are multiple types of options with different tax implications, and the results depend in part on whether you keep or sell the company stock.

WORKING DURING RETIREMENT

At first this might seem like a contradiction in terms. Doesn't retirement mean that you are not working? Not necessarily. Perhaps you are working only part-time or are part of a phased retirement program. Or working and not getting paid for it (it's called volunteering).

Working for pay can not only provide some retirement income, but it can also provide you with more income later on. From the investment standpoint, when you earn income from working, you do not have to tap into your savings as much and your investments have more time to grow. You may even be able to save some of the money you earn. You will then have more investments to draw from later on.

A part-time job can lead to increased future Social Security payments in two ways. First, you may be able to postpone filing for benefits. Remember, waiting to file increases the size of the benefit every year until age seventy. Second, each year you work has the potential to replace lower income from the past and become a part of your highest thirty-five years when the amount of the benefit is calculated, even if you are already collecting or past age seventy.

You can find a variety of ways to work part-time, particularly if the work is in the same company or field as your previous full-time job. The most straightforward is to arrange to work or continue working at a regular time each week, perhaps some whole days each week or parts of each day. If there is a busy season for the firm, you may be able to arrange seasonal work then.

Another approach is to work as a substitute to temporarily replace workers who are sick or on vacation. You can work for longer stretches of time, perhaps weeks or months, if you arrange to work on particular projects. Consulting may be available too, where you contract to work with multiple firms in your area of expertise.

Sometimes paid work is coupled with volunteer work. An organization may have the funds to support some kinds of activities but not others. The work and volunteering combination is one way for you to earn some income and provide extra leverage for the contributions that you make to an organization.

Sometimes part-time work can be scheduled at a faraway location. For example, you might decide to teach English in France over the summer and then return to your home, only to continue the international travel and teaching somewhere else at another time.

Maybe you would like to work at something entirely different in retirement from what you did earlier. Such work may satisfy your curiosity, express a long-time unfulfilled interest, or allow you to contribute in different ways or for different reasons.

If you define retirement as the time when you are doing more of what you want to do and less of what you do not want to do, then your goal should be to find work that you really love to do. Even if the pay is less, your life will be enriched.

INCOME FROM ROYALTIES

Perhaps you have a patented invention that is valuable to someone else's business, and they will pay you for its use. Perhaps you have written a book, and the publisher will pay you a percentage of sales. Your compensation from past inventions could augment your retirement income, even though you are not working. However, royalties often have limited lifetimes before technology or people's interests move on to something newer.

SELLING SOMETHING VALUABLE

You may own assets that could be converted into income during retirement. Here are some examples of ways to tap into their value.

Consider your home if you have equity in it. You can directly or indirectly convert it into income by two ways. One is to sell your home and live in a less expensive one. The second is to obtain a reverse mortgage, which will provide you with a stream of income or a pool of money to be invested.

If you own a profitable business and will no longer be working in it during your retirement, you may be able to sell it. However, the business must consist of more than you and your role in it. If your business now depends entirely on you, you may be able to transform it into something of value to someone else. That process might take years to accomplish, but the rewards could be substantial.

Other assets that you may be able to sell include a second piece of property, an extra car, a boat, valuable artwork, or jewelry. You may also have the option of renting out property instead of selling.

LARGESSE FROM FAMILY AND FRIENDS

Living on the kindness of friends and relatives is much less dire than it sounds. Long before the growth of single-family homes, people lived with their extended families. Even today young adults move in with their parents, particularly if they are having a difficult time finding a job. The parents provide shelter and sometimes food for free for the son or daughter.

Sometimes parents move in with their children. This is one way that children can provide support for their parents—physical, mental, and economic. Sometimes the benefit is mutual, for example, when the parents watch over their grandchildren while the middle generation works.

Sometimes friends decide to share a living space. At the least, costs for shelter for each person can be substantially reduced. Or sometimes an apartment renter or homeowner may permit someone to stay with them for free. Sometimes this arrangement is coupled with care being provided of the home, homeowners' pets, or other family members. This approach can present challenges, particularly if the renter or homeowner values privacy, but sometimes this can be a win-win for everyone.

Another source of retirement income can be an inheritance, if you are lucky enough to have been born into a family that has accumulated some wealth. That wealth may have to be shared with siblings upon the death of parents. Of course, for the inheritance to provide retirement income, it must be set aside for that purpose and managed properly.

ANNIE AND DOUG WORK OUT A DEAL

Annie continues to think about joining the Peace Corps. She is not sure what she can do with her home and all of her belongings while she is gone.

Doug is starting to think that he may need to make some serious changes in his life, including starting to put some money aside for retirement. He is not sure where that money will come from.

Doug and Annie may be able to help each other. Doug could move into Annie's place if she will be away for a few years. If Doug doesn't pay rent, he can use the money he is saving to contribute to a retirement plan for himself at work. Doug will get a tax break if he uses this approach. Every additional $1.50 that he contributes to his retirement plan pretax will reduce his take-home pay by only $1.00. He would effectively get a $1.50 benefit for every dollar it costs him.

Perhaps, Annie might even pay Doug a small amount to take care of her affairs while she is gone.

What Annie gets from all of this is the assurance that all of her belongings and maybe some of her affairs will be taken care of while she is gone. Plus she loves Doug and will be thrilled to help him in his venture to retire someday. Sometimes arrangements like this just happen, especially if you are looking for them.

JUGGLING INCOME

Retirement, it turns out, has several financial stages. Social Security and required minimum distributions (RMDs) from retirement plans are both age-related. Your full retirement age may trigger the time you file for your own or spousal Social Security benefits.

RMDS are triggered when you reach the age of seventy and a half. You can start taking your RMDs in the year you turn seventy and a half. Or you can wait until April 1 of the year *after* you reach that age to take withdrawals from your IRAs and some retirement plans. You calculate the amount according to the IRA Uniform Lifetime Table. If you wait to take out the RMDs to the year after you turn seventy and a half, then you have to take two years' worth of withdrawals that year. You will pay income tax on the withdrawals in the year following the distribution.

Receiving RMDs triggers the income taxes you pay. Many people end up using the RMDs as income to live off. You can invest any RMD money that you do not need in your personal accounts if you like.

So from a cash-flow standpoint, you may draw on nonretirement money until RMD money becomes available. If you retire in your sixties, you may have a gap between earning money from working and receiving the two sources of income (RMDs and Social Security) at age seventy. The way to bridge the gap is to use money you have saved, particularly personal savings, to tide you over until you reach seventy.

Where does paid work fit into the timing? You can work for pay in early or late retirement. Earlier is easier—both to find the work and to do the work. Deciding what and when to start the different income streams is a puzzle for you to solve.

CATHY AND CHUCK THINK ABOUT FUTURE INCOME

Chuck and Cathy have been receiving their income from their business for years. It is hard for them to imagine it any other way. They know that their cash flow and income may be different in the future, partly because Courtney may take over the business at some point. Will they be paid dividends as business owners, or salaries as employees, or fees as consultants? Do they really want to act like bankers to their children—get paid by their children from restaurant profits?  What if things go wrong? Right now most of their cash flow is being used to pay down their debt on the new restaurants they are opening. Where will the money come from?

Business transitions are a delicate process. The business can be

 like the goose laying the golden eggs. They have to be careful with the goose, or the eggs will stop. Cathy and Chuck could set up a pension plan of some type for themselves to provide another source of income in retirement.

PREPARING FOR SOCIAL SECURITY, WORKING AND OTHER RETIREMENT INCOME

You will be better prepared for retirement if you evaluate each of these sources of income:

- Social Security has its twists and turns if you are or have been married. Articles on the topic will make you aware of the issues, but there is no substitute to "running the numbers" to compare your alternatives.
- Check with current and past employers to identify pensions and other benefit plans. Learn what your choices are in preparation for making decisions in this area.
- If you want to continue working part-time for your current employer, then you may want to pursue that as part of arrangements for retiring. What do you need to do to make that happen? If you want to work someplace else, there is no substitute for networking with friends and acquaintances to learn of opportunities.

Just as you should be thinking about your expenses during retirement, you should put together a package of retirement incomes. This information can become a part of your budgeting process.

15. The Right Investment Ingredients

Over the last five to twenty years there has been an explosion in the number of investment alternatives available to retail investors, and the menu is growing all the time. Some of the newcomers, involving financial derivatives, come from recent financial inventions. Some of the largest of them are called hedge funds. Others have been available to wealthy investors for centuries. Computers have made them possible to break down into smaller pieces which retail investors can purchase. It is important to know about the full menu of investment alternatives you have so that you can more effectively diversify your portfolio, thereby reducing risk and increasing your investment returns.

While working, you probably used your 401(k), 403(b), or other retirement plans to accumulate savings. Your investment choices were probably limited and at least partly preselected for you. For example, most pension plans include many variations of U.S. large-company stock funds but not many foreign or developing market or smaller companies. Most nonstock, nonbond investments are not available in retirement plans. Once you retire and roll your retirement plans into your IRAs, you have many more choices. Your new investments could be less expensive and provide better diversification for you.

If your investments are to function as an engine for income during your retirement, you want that engine to work efficiently and effectively. The efficiency of your investment portfolio comes from having the right components in the right mix so that they work well together. Some of the effectiveness of your investments will come from using the tax laws for your benefit.

What investment choices will you have? How do they work? How do you choose the most appropriate ones for you?

THE ROLE OF STOCKS IN YOUR INVESTMENT PORTFOLIO

One key advantage of owning stocks is the ease of buying, holding, and selling them through brokerage houses. Hundreds of millions, even billions, of identical shares from the same company may be available to trade on the stock exchanges. You can easily price them and purchase a mix of shares of different companies to include in your investment mix.

Stocks and growth. Stocks will be one of the most important fuel sources for your investment engine. You include stocks, which are nothing more than part ownership of corporations, for their possibility of growth. You can generate some income from the dividends that come from their earnings. But they frequently reinvest some of their earnings for more growth. If they are successful in growing, their earnings and dividends may also grow. When that happens, the stock value may increase. Historically, the average returns over long periods of time—growth in stock value plus dividends—have substantially exceeded the rate of inflation and the returns on bonds and cash. Coupled with that higher return is, of course, higher risk over shorter time periods than you would have with many other classes of investments. Not only can returns be lower than expected for years, but they can even be negative.

Some people are more optimistic than others. The optimists argue that stocks are all you need to own, because historically "in the long run" they have produced the highest returns. They believe that the economy will have its ups and downs. They say, just hang in there.

The counterargument is that we live now in exceptional times, and the future may not be as great as the past, when stocks have had average returns in the range of 10 percent per year. After all, when you read the newspapers, you know about the risks of owning stocks in these difficult times with so many problems—the business cycle, employment, shrinking manufacturing, the Fed, economies overseas doing too well or not well enough, the value of the dollar, changes in interest rates, overvalued stocks, politics here and abroad, war, and natural disasters. With all of that going on, do you really want to and can you afford to take those risks, particularly now?

Actually, similar risks have always been around and probably always will be. Stocks have increased in value in spite of the risks, because of the growth of corporate earnings.

Is there a force that will continue to propel the value of stocks even higher in the long run? Yes, I believe there is: technology, another term for human creativity. It is hard to see a time when we will run out of ideas, when discovery and creativity will diminish. If anything, the rate of progress is increasing around the world.

Companies will continue to sell more goods and services. Consumption continues as you replace items when they wear out. You may also purchase items because they are better than the old ones. Demand for products and services will also increase around the world as the population and the middle classes continue to grow.

Does this mean that all stocks will increase in value in the long run? Absolutely not. In fact, of the twenty-five thousand-plus companies traded publicly from 1926 to 2015, only thirty of them, the superstars, accounted for a third of all of the growth of the economy. In fact, most publicly traded companies have lost money over their lifetimes. Only in retrospect can you identify the superstars.

Competition among companies is particularly brutal when an

industry is young and expanding rapidly. Initial profitability attracts other companies as competitors, and most of them go broke.

Classification of stocks. The total number of U.S. stocks listed on major U.S. exchanges now is approximately five thousand. Foreign companies listed on their own exchanges are at least double that number.

There are different ways to classify those companies and their stocks. Companies are in different industries. Some companies are large, others are small. Some are fast growing, others not. Growth of the companies has varied all over the map and changes substantially from year to year.

Stocks and other investments are categorized into what are called asset classes. The most commonly discussed and tracked asset class is *large-cap stocks*, the largest U.S. companies. These are reported daily through two indices: the Dow Jones Industrial Average, which contains twenty of the largest companies, and the Standard and Poor's 500, which tracks the five hundred largest publicly traded companies.

This asset class can be subdivided into two others: *U.S. large-cap growth* and *U.S. large-cap value*, the faster-growing and the more stable companies. Another example of an asset class is *U.S. small-cap value*, which contains those small (perhaps less than $4 billion in value) companies located in the United States that are more stable. They have not been growing rapidly and can be purchased at lower prices.

REAL ESTATE AS A DIRECT INVESTMENT

Direct ownership of real estate is another type of investment, an asset class, which can provide you with a retirement income from rents. When you sell your property, you will also have a capital gain or loss, depending on what has happened to the value of your property.

The force propelling property values to increase is ultimately the increase in human population with a fixed amount of land to service the population. The buildings, however, change value from the supply of and demand for comparable properties. This in turn is affected by economic factors, including the state of the general economy, technology disruptions to corporations, and interest rates.

Direct ownership of real estate is more problematic than owning stocks. Each piece of property is unique and difficult to price since it is not traded often. Selling individual properties is generally difficult and expensive. You usually have to sell the whole property, even if you need a fraction of the value. It can take considerable time to sell real estate, whereas stocks can be bought or sold in seconds on the stock exchange on any business day.

Owning real estate directly is more like owning your own business. You need to collect the rents and maintain the property yourself, unless you hire someone else to do that for you. If you hire someone, you have to pay them, so your profitability decreases. Yet you still have the ultimate responsibility for the property if something goes wrong.

BRIAN AND THE OIL WELL

Brian's younger brother has offered to cut him into an oil well in North Dakota that he manages. It has huge potential because it is in between two other wells that have been big producers. Brian and Becky have had little experience with investments and none with investments like this. He and Becky are not sure how feasible it would be for them to participate and how such an investment would affect their retirement plans.

Private ventures like this have the same risk as running a business, except more so. There are so many factors out of Brian's control.

To be successful, the well has to find sufficient oil, bring it out of the earth economically, and sell it at a profit, possibly over decades.

Participation in any private venture has huge risks associated with it. But Brian is in a personal situation with even more risk than usual. Brian has no cash to invest. He would have to cash in all his retirement plans, pay taxes on them, and invest the remaining after-tax amount. He would be putting all his eggs in one basket. If this investment did not work out, through no fault of his own, they might have to put off their retirement for decades.

GOLD AND COMMODITIES AS AN INVESTMENT

You can own gold bars, pork bellies, or a variety of other commodities. Their price is affected by supply and demand for the commodity. To own some of them, you have to pay to store them. There is no inherent force that will increase their value, and it may be difficult for you to generate income from them, because they do not pay dividends.

CONTRACTS (CASH, BONDS, FUTURES, AND OPTIONS) AS AN INVESTMENT

Bonds are contracts. Here is how the *contract* works. When you buy a bond, you in effect lend money to a corporation or government organization. In return, the organization *contracts* to pay you a dividend, frequently semiannually, until maturity. At some predetermined maturity date, it will pay you your money back. Riskier organizations, those having money problems or lower credit ratings, and longer-term maturities pay you more because of the higher risk. Bond prices are frequently less volatile than stocks but can fluctuate with changing interest rates and with changes in the credit worthiness of the organizations. Will they be able to pay you back?

Bonds can have long or short maturities, with interest paid by organizations that are financially strong or weak; they can be domestic or foreign. Different bond types are sometimes considered to be different asset classes. The riskiest of these—long-term bonds issued by problem organizations—have historically had, on average, the highest return. There are many more bonds available than stocks because each corporation or government entity may at different times issue different bonds. You may want to include bonds in your investment mix because they offer lower potential risk than stocks and a regular steady income.

Cash includes paper money and coins. But the same term is frequently used to describe bank accounts, which are nothing more than *contracts* with banks. They are the most stable and frequently the lowest paying of the alternatives. However, cash is safe, partly because of government FDIC insurance, and it is also liquid, that is, accessible. Longer-term cash in the form of certificates of deposits is less liquid and higher paying.

A futures *contract* requires you as the owner to buy or sell commodities or investments at a particular price and future time. These contracts generally have very high leverage and huge risks. They require constant attention because of rapid price changes. Unless you own them with related investments, it is possible to lose all of your money. When owned without related investments, they are *not* suitable as retirement investments.

Options are similar to futures. They are *contracts* that permit, but do not require, you to buy or sell an investment at a particular price in the future. If you own options without other related investments, they too can be particularly risky but offer a high potential return. If they are coupled with other investments, they can "hedge" (limit) the risk. In fact, hedge funds may own them.

For example, if you own an option to sell a hundred shares of Apple stock at $210 a share over the next six months and the price of an Apple share is $215, then the options are worth at maturity $5 × 100 = $500. You can buy at $210 and use the option to sell at $215. If the price goes to $215, the options are worthless, because you would not want to buy shares at $215 and use the option to sell them at $210 each. But if you own both the options and the stock, the option will provide a hedge (cushion) for your investment. If your stock price falls and you lose money on the stock, the option will permit you to make the money back from the appreciation of the option value itself.

CHOOSING INDIVIDUAL INVESTMENTS

Timing. The trick is figuring out what and when to buy and sell. Can you really identify and purchase bargains? The research says no, that the price of any security reflects all of the information available about it at that time. As news becomes available and expectations change about the future profitability of a company, then investors immediately buy or sell the security to take the new information into account, sometimes within a fraction of a second. By the time you get your information, it is literally old news.

Picking the right investments. Newsletters, television, and of course the internet will advise you what investments to purchase and when to buy and sell. But objective analysis of these sources has shown that on average following their advice does not provide a higher return than throwing darts at a newspaper to select investments.

Obviously, you could just buy the "good" investments, the ones that have had outstanding performance in the past. Such investments are expensive, which means that you pay a lot for a dollar's earnings because you expect those earnings to increase substantially in the future. These are called growth stocks. The companies that have not done so well in the past are called value stocks, and they are cheaper because expectations are so low.

The research. If there were no surprises and the strong always got stronger and the weaker always got weaker, then buying only growth stocks would work well. So how many surprises are there? Eugene Fama, from the University of Chicago, did the research, for which he was awarded the Nobel Prize in Economics in 2013. The answer is that there are many surprises. On average, over time, value stocks outperform growth stocks! And on average smaller companies outperform larger ones. More recently, Fama has demonstrated that more profitable companies outperform less profitable ones; in other words, promises without performance go just so far.

The link between risk and returns is not accidental. Consider two investments with the same rate of return but with one having much more risk than the other. Of course, you would choose the investment with the lower risk. The only reason that you would choose the investment with the higher risk is if it offered a higher potential rate of return.

That does not mean that risk always pays off, particularly in the short run. It means that if you include investments that have a higher risk, you should do so carefully and thoughtfully and that you do your best to manage and contain that risk. In the long run it may well pay off.

Research has also shown that costs matter. Lower-cost investments on average outperform higher-cost ones. Buying and holding individual securities is the least expensive way to invest if you do it all yourself. You have to pay only the trading cost at the brokerage house. However, if you do a lot of trading, those trading costs will mount up and subtract from your returns.

The road forward will always have bumps—wars, natural disasters, changes in the economy, and so on. An investor can easily get discouraged. But the volatility of investments can offer investors opportunities to buy low and sell high.

The economist John Maynard Keynes said that in the long run of investing we will all be dead. There is no certainty that investing will pay off. But removing all of the risk almost certainly dooms us to a life with lost opportunities for ourselves and our communities.

ANNIE EXPLORES INVESTMENT CLUBS

Annie wants to take an active role in managing her own investments. Some of her new friends, who are also widows, are starting an investment club. Each member will invest a token amount of money each month and be responsible for researching an investment opportunity

and presenting it to the group. Annie is looking forward to the social part of the group as well as the opportunity to learn more.

Investment clubs can be a great way to meet other investors and learn more about choosing investments, about different businesses and sectors of the economy, and about economics. As to making money—not so much. At the least, Annie will learn to appreciate that investing is not as easy as it may look.

Annie should be careful not to draw conclusions about investing in general from her experiences with the group. The investment club portfolio will be much less diversified than any index, and its performance can differ substantially from the index, up or down. Much of the club's performance will come from the luck of its choices, good or bad.

INVESTMENT POOLS

Instead of owning individual stocks, bonds, and so on, you can buy pools of investments. Investment pools have many advantages over direct ownership of individual investments:

1. *Professional management.* They are managed daily by teams of highly skilled professionals who buy and sell investments and provide periodic reports. You are in a sense hiring help.
2. *Diversification.* They hold many investments at the same time—from dozens to thousands. They can be homogeneous—all of the same asset class—or they can contain multiple types of investments.
3. *Objectives.* They have goals such as type of investments to be

included and excluded, objectives (e.g., growth or income), and methodologies for accomplishing their objectives.

4. *Small scale.* They can be purchased in small amounts and thus work well for investors with small amounts of money. Even a small investor can achieve diversification.

5. *Access to other investments.* Many alternative investments are available in small amounts that are not otherwise available.

The best-known pool is the mutual fund. Its more common variation is open end. This means that shares are created or redeemed at the end of the day at the mutual fund company when investors buy or sell shares. The less common variation is closed end. It has a fixed number of shares and is traded like a stock anytime the exchange is open.

There are many other pools of investments, each with its own acronym. These include REITSs, BDCs, ETFs, MLPs, and VAs. The table on page 156 gives a brief overview of types of pooled investments, the kinds of investments they hold, and their features.

Mutual funds, the first of these investment pools, were invented in the eighteenth century. The first modern U.S. mutual fund was invented in the 1920s. There were 100 mutual funds in the 1950s. Now there are more than 10,000 unique funds and 25,000 variations in the United States alone. Mutual funds and their relatives can own any of the asset classes described earlier in this chapter or mixes of them. Funds can also own other not-yet-mentioned asset classes.

REITs are real estate investment trusts that hold real estate investments. REITs can be publicly traded or privately held. They provide ownership of commercial properties, including office buildings, stores, apartments, hotels, resorts, warehouses, and many others. Multiple properties are generally bundled into a single REIT. More recently some mutual funds have also been developed to hold and manage real estate investments and publicly traded REITs.

BDCs, or business development companies, hold many loans to smaller and privately held businesses that frequently have a difficult time obtaining loans or cannot afford to issue corporate bonds. Loans are generally safer than bonds from the same company because

TYPES OF POOLED INVESTMENTS

Type	Kinds of investments	Features
Mutual fund – open end	Most frequently stocks, bonds or other contracts, real estate plus some other individual securities, or combinations of them	Bought and sold daily; price is exact value of contents at close of trading
Mutual fund – closed end	Same as open-end mutual funds	Bought and sold all day on stock exchange, like stocks, for a price determined by supply and demand; could be higher or lower than the value of the contents
Exchange traded fund (ETF)	Similar to mutual funds	Traded on exchanges at premium or discount; buy-and-hold approach
Real estate investment trust (REIT)	Real estate properties of all kinds	Can be traded (on stock exchange) or nontraded; authorized by Investment Act of 1940, like mutual funds
Business development corporation (BDC)	Loans to private or small corporations	Authorized by Investment Act of 1940, like mutual funds and REITs
Master limited partnership (MLP)	Oil and gas properties	Some tax advantages
Variable annuity (VA), Variable life insurance (VLI)—both have separate accounts	Mutual fund–like investments	Investments inside annuity or life insurance contracts; tax-deferred growth

they are paid off before bonds if the issuing company runs into trouble. Loans have collateral backing them up; bonds do not. These corporate loans are often in the millions of dollars, so they are not purchased by the typical investor. But purchasing shares of a BDC makes them affordable and available.

Three other pooled investments are ETFs (exchange traded funds), MLPs (master limited partnerships), and VAs (variable annuities). ETFs are similar to mutual funds but are actively traded like a stock. ETFs frequently take a buy-and-hold approach, so they are known for their low costs. MLPs hold oil and gas wells and components of energy distribution, such as pipelines and refineries.

VAs are managed by insurance companies, not investment or mutual fund companies. In some senses they are hybrid products. VAs have separate accounts similar to mutual funds. And they may contain contracts that permit annuitizing: income for life, subject to the insurance company having the ability to live up to the terms of the contracts. The contracts may contain a death benefit as well.

The professionals managing the pools use a variety of processes to identify which investments to purchase. Some actively manage the contents of their pools. They use "fundamental" analysis, such as interviewing CEOs and other corporate management and in-depth reviews of the companies' balance sheets and economic trends. Others identify prospective companies to purchase through "technical" analysis, such as review of past price movements or databases to compare different features of the companies.

Many pooled investments specialize by investing in a single asset class or even sector of the economy, for example, utility companies. Some are more restricted in what they can invest in, others have more flexibility. The investment guidelines and processes, costs, risks, and history are all described in a prospectus for the investments, which you are supposed to read before purchasing the investment.

ALTERNATIVE INVESTMENTS

The newest types of investments are sometimes called *alternative investments*. They are generally more expensive than a typical stock mutual fund because they are more complicated to manage. There are a huge range of these, but many of them make money from one of three approaches: use of futures contracts and options, derivatives, and arbitrage.

Derivatives are more common than you think. Derivatives include futures contracts and options. Their value is derived from the value or performance of another investment. An example is an investment that is hedged, e.g., stocks whose large volatility is reduced by coupling it with options that limit gains and losses.

Arbitrage classically means buying one investment and simultaneously selling a related one. The relationship between the two investments could be in time (buying an asset now and contracting to sell it later), buying "good" stocks (or bonds or real estate) now and selling "bad" ones at the same time, buying and selling two currencies or commodities, or buying and selling companies that will be merging. Because of the hedging, they are typically much less risky than buying the underlying investments themselves (e.g., stocks).

Many of these alternative approaches are now available in a mutual fund format. They have become more popular as a tool to diversify traditional investments of stocks, bonds, cash, and real estate.

COSTS FOR POOLED INVESTMENTS

Professional investment management is not free. Annual management costs are disclosed in the investment prospectus and frequently range from nearly 0 to 1.5 percent per year. Costs are higher for specialty funds, like alternatives or harder to research areas, like companies in emerging markets. They may be lower for bond funds or funds with less active management.

You pay up to three additional costs when you own investments. One is the cost for trading securities inside a pooled investment. Since the typical actively managed fund buys and sells 90 percent of its assets each year, that trading cost approximates another 1 percent each year. It is not disclosed in the prospectus. Another cost, typically 0.25 percent per year, is called the 12b-1 fee, which pays the sales person. Still another cost is for the help you get in selecting and managing your investment if you hire a professional; it can range from 1 percent each year to a onetime cost of up to 7 percent.

A no-load fund is one you buy directly from the investment company. You pay only the management and trading costs but not buying or selling costs that would otherwise go to an agent who helped you select the fund. You can purchase even less expensive institutional funds wholesale through a fee-based financial advisor, who can bundle purchases for multiple clients together and purchase investments that normally require $500,000 to $1,000,000 or more to be invested.

These costs may seem high to you, but what is your alternative? The research that the management does is generally much more extensive than you can do yourself. They have the skills and time to do it. They can spread their costs over a large pool of money invested with them.

CHOOSING POOLED INVESTMENTS

Like choosing individual investments, this is harder than it looks. The obvious approach is to choose pooled investments with the best past performance. The extra performance should come from the value added by the investment management team and their research processes.

Performance data are readily available. They are even standardized; funds are required to report net returns after all costs for year-to-date, one year, five years, ten years, and over the lifetime of the fund. This standardization makes it easy to compare one fund to another.

You can also compare performance to a benchmark. The most commonly used benchmark is the Standard and Poor's 500 index, which tracks the performance of the five hundred largest companies publicly traded in the United States. All asset classes have at least one accepted benchmark.

You would think and hope that the returns of professionally

managed pools would exceed their relevant benchmarks. On average, they don't—70 to 80 percent of the time they underperform. Mutual fund families frequently hide their poor performances by merging funds with the lowest returns into funds with higher returns and keeping the track record of only the fund with the higher return.

Still you might think that you could choose a fund with an excellent track record over the past five to ten years. As long as the same fund managers are in place, then you would expect that the fund would outperform the average fund. Here is what the research says about this. The performance of funds with the poorest returns tends to repeat itself, so you should avoid those. A small proportion of funds with excellent track records do repeat their outstanding performance, but it is impossible to tell in advance which funds those will be.

Fund ratings do not work. Firms like Morningstar, Forbes, and others rate mutual funds. Their ratings are generally in disagreement with each other.

How can the fund managers be so ineffective? Predicting is hard. Fund managers are smart, but all have access to the same information. Their active management generally means picking a small subset of securities in their asset class, which may or may not include the super stocks that generate a substantial fraction of the market's total return.

Managing securities actively is expensive. Research studies have shown that there is an approximate inverse relationship between fund costs and performance. This means that expensive funds do not do as well as inexpensive ones.

All of these factors have driven investors more and more to purchase index funds, which use a buy-and-hold approach to purchase securities that mimic an index, a benchmark. They are much less expensive to manage.

Index fund managers are paid to mimic their benchmark index as closely as possible. So when the composition of the index changes, as it must do periodically, they all buy and sell the same stocks at the same time. This does add some cost to the process of managing the fund, which gets buried in the performance figures.

FIDUCIARY SCORE

With all of these caveats about picking and using mutual funds to give you access to the investments you want to include in your mix, what can you use to evaluate the quality of investments in an objective way? The answer is the Fiduciary Score, which summarizes the factors you should consider. Here are those factors:

- Performance compared to peers
- Risk (volatility) compared to peers. Less is better.
- Costs compared to peers. Less is better.
- Size, preferably larger than $100 million. Otherwise the fixed costs of managing the fund will affect future performance.
- Registration. Mutual funds are well regulated, but other investment pools, such as partnerships, may not be. Regulation protects you as a consumer.
- Management team. It should have been in place for at least two years. If not, what do past risk and performance really mean?
- Consistency. How closely are the fund managers following their guidelines for what to include in the fund? Some funds buy what is hot. In that case, you never know what you really own at any one time.
- Correlation. If the fund says that it contains, for example, smaller U.S. companies, does it go up and down at the same time as other funds of the same type? If not, the fund may have an odd mix of investments, which could vastly over- or underperform that asset class.

PREPARING FOR INVESTMENTS IN RETIREMENT

When you retire and move your investments to IRAs where you can control your investments yourself, you will have many more investment possibilities to choose from. So your preparation for retirement should include educating yourself about investments—what investments are out there and how you can separate the good from the not so good. You may get some ideas from talking with friends and relatives, but books and professionals will probably be the most useful.

With your newfound skills, you will find it helpful to review your current investments. Some you may choose to keep, others to replace when you set up your investments to provide retirement income to you.

16. The Right Investment Mix

Unfortunately, you are not done after you have identified suitable potential investments to include in your portfolio. You still have to decide what mix of those investments is appropriate for you. For example, if you choose a mix for its higher return and higher risk, then it will be comprised primarily of stocks. A more conservative mix will have fewer stocks.

During the past several decades the court system has gotten involved in defining what investments are appropriate for advisors to recommend to investors. This has come about because of lawsuits brought by beneficiaries of trusts against trustees for mismanaging their investments, and against employers managing pensions. The courts developed the Prudent Investor Rule, which says that the money manager is required to invest like a prudent investor would.

When this has been spelled out in the court cases, three requirements are mentioned the most:

- Investments should be diversified.
- Lower-cost investments should be used rather than higher-cost ones.

- Passively managed investments (buy-and-hold) are more appropriate than actively managed ones.

These three requirements have been expanded and developed into the Fiduciary Score described in detail in Chapter 15. Costs and trading are disclosed in an investment prospectus.

Diversification requires a more detailed discussion.

DIVERSIFICATION

Would you categorize a diet made up exclusively of several scoops of ice cream, each with a different flavor, to be balanced? No. So too, you need a real variety of investments to have an effective and balanced investment mix.

Clearly, you do not want to have all of your eggs in one basket. Since your objectives change in retirement from making and growing money to keeping the money you have already accumulated, it is important to manage not just for investment return but also for risk in the process. By having a diverse mix of investments, you protect yourself from overconfidently making bets on "sure things," which do not always work out as expected.

Not all mixes are equally effective. You want your investments to work together efficiently. And you want them to work effectively for you in particular.

An extreme example of an undiversified portfolio is one that contains primarily company stock that you might own from a previous job. Depending too strongly on the fortunes of a single company is hazardous to the success of your retirement. Overconcentration of investments is a risk not worth taking; you will not necessarily be rewarded by higher returns, and you will have all that extra risk. Even if a stock has had outstanding performance in the past, there is no guarantee that the higher return will continue in the future.

EFFICIENT MIXES AND MODERN PORTFOLIO THEORY

Nobel Prize winner Harry Markowitz developed Modern Portfolio Theory, which shows that some portfolio mixes work better than others. Some mixes are more efficient than others; that is, they give more bang for the buck.

Using historical data, you can determine a return and a risk level (volatility) associated with each portfolio mix. If you were to look at different mixes, you would find that for each risk level, there is a mix of components that has had the highest return. Or conversely for each return, there is a mix of the components that have had the lowest risk.

You would also see that as you add risk to a portfolio of investments, the returns also increase but not proportionally. You reach a point of diminishing returns, where adding substantial risk adds only a small additional return. So this level of risk is just not worth it.

Before Markowitz's research, this was not obvious. You can calculate the past return of a portfolio from a weighted average of the returns of its components. For example, if over a period of years stocks returned 9 percent per year, and bonds returned 3 percent per year, and your mix of investments was two-thirds stock and one-third bonds, then you can calculate the return of your portfolio to be $(9\% \times 2/3) + (3\% \times 1/3) = 6\% + 1\% = 7$ percent.

However, this approach does not work for calculating the risk level of a portfolio. The risks associated with a mix are less than you might think. If the components are truly different from each other, then the changes in their prices are not correlated with each other. Thus, the price of one component may be increasing while another is decreasing in value some of the time. The changes, which are a measure of risk, tend to cancel out some of the fluctuations and risks as compared to the components themselves. This is the closest you will ever get to getting something for nothing in the investment field.

If the prices of two investments move in the same direction all of the time, then they are perfectly correlated. If they always move in opposite directions, then they are negatively correlated. In the real world, correlations are never perfect, and sometimes correlations between investments change.

For a portfolio with many components, the calculations of risk are complex and are done via computer. The most efficient portfolios are ones that contain quite different components, that is, that are highly diversified.

If you were to do the calculations of risk for portfolios of many investment components, you would learn lessons about what effective and ineffective diversification really is. Here are some conclusions from the calculations:

- It is possible to have too much of a good thing. Yes, stocks have historically had higher returns than bonds or cash. Yes, if you increase the proportion of stock in a portfolio from 70 to 100 percent, you will increase the returns of your portfolio proportionally. But the risks go way up.
- Broadening the composition of your portfolio works. If you include smaller companies in addition to larger ones in your portfolio, not only will your returns increase, but the risks will not increase as much because the two asset classes are not completely correlated.
- If you include really different asset classes in your portfolio, such as alternative investments, they may be particularly effective in managing risk in your portfolio as a whole. They can increase the returns of a portfolio, reduce risk, or both. The more different they are, that is, not correlated in price movement with stocks, bonds, and cash, the more effective they will be. You may not need a lot of them to have a well-diversified portfolio.

MIXES EFFECTIVE FOR YOU

To have a portfolio that will work effectively, you must deal with two major issues. The first is overcoming the natural tendency for individual investors to underperform the market. The second is finding an investment approach that works for you and your circumstances—a personal investing plan.

Underperformance and behavioral finance. For decades, the research firm Dalbar has analyzed the annual investment performance of stocks and bonds, both for the investments themselves and for the retail investors who own them. Typically, investors underperform by 3 to 5 percent each year for the same investments! How can this be?

Individual investors tend to buy and sell investments at the wrong time. They buy investments when they are optimistic about future performance—after they have had good performance—and sell investments when they are pessimistic—after they have declined in value. This is the buy high/sell low approach.

Economists, such as Nobel Prize–winning Daniel Kahneman, have opened up a whole new field, called behavioral finance, to understand this investor behavior. Economists and psychologists have shown that a number of irrational attitudes contribute to these behaviors, including the following:

- *Overconfidence.* This leads to overweighting and underweighting investments in a portfolio based in part on false memories. You may tend to remember predictions you made that worked out well but forget those that did not. This is Monday-morning quarterbacking. It can convince you to buy the "best" stocks at the "right" time.
- *Overoptimism and overpessimism.* This belief is that whatever has happened recently will continue indefinitely. It may continue but probably not indefinitely.
- *Herding.* This behavior is following the crowd, who after all know what is going to happen and why—or not.
- *Overexplanation.* In the short-term, price changes are random. Yet newscasters attach meaning to everything to explain those changes.
- *Investing in the familiar.* Why is it familiar? Don't other people also know about this? Hasn't this information already been considered in the price of the investment?

You as an investor will be able to overcome these behaviors by having a plan and executing it.

Your personal investing plan. No single portfolio works for everybody. An effective portfolio for you must not contain more risk and volatility than you can live with. So ideally, your preparation for retirement includes constructing an investment portfolio with the highest return compatible with your risk tolerance.

Operationally, there are two approaches to measuring the risk that you are prepared to take. One is to answer the questions in a risk profile questionnaire. Many of these questionnaires are available on the internet or through financial advisors.

The questions are similar to the following: When will you need to have access to and spend your investment money? How do you feel about changes in your investment values? How will changes in investments affect your investment behavior? You generally have a few choices for the answers.

If you choose answers that indicate that you are prepared to or need to tolerate more risk, then you have a higher risk tolerance. The higher risk tolerance translates to a riskier portfolio, one that contains more stock. Lower tolerance translate to less stock.

You may be identified as a "conservative," "balanced," "growth," or "aggressive" investor, and an appropriate portfolio is recommended to you. Such designations may be in the range of 30 percent, 60 percent, 75 percent, or 90 percent stock, respectively, with other investments comprising the rest of your portfolio. You choose the mix to be compatible with your risk level and the highest return possible for that risk level. This is the most common approach to choosing a portfolio.

The second, more sophisticated approach for building and choosing a portfolio is available only through financial advisors who use it as part of their investment planning process. It involves first figuring out how much volatility you can accept, perhaps over a six-month period; in other words, how big a loss in your investment portfolio can you sustain without doing something foolish, like selling low. You can estimate the maximum loss as a percentage of the investments you have accumulated, but a more effective measure may be to translate that into actual dollars that you can accept as a loss.

To use this second approach, you take three steps to build an investment portfolio, starting with the mix of investments that you currently have:

1. Determine the ideal amount of risk that you are prepared to take. This step is a little scary, but you might as well start with the most critical issue up front. You start with an initial rough estimate of the maximum amount of money that you are prepared to lose in a six-month period. Then you tweak this by comparing a wide range of mixes and seeing the trade-off between risk and return. For example, are you willing to improve your initial portfolio by accepting an additional maximum fall in value of $30,000—worst case—if that portfolio could generate an additional maximum gain of $50,000—best case? This process is equivalent to trying on many clothes and seeing what fits best. The end result is a risk score, the amount of risk that you are prepared to take with your investments.

2. Measure the amount of risk that you have in your current portfolio. Your mix of investments has an estimated return based on past returns, and it also has a risk score associated with it.

3. Tinker with the portfolio mix. There are two important reasons to do this. The first is to bring the current mix with its associated risk score closer to your ideal risk score from step 1 above. The second is to optimize your portfolio mix by substituting a variety of investments to determine how they affect the projected return, risk, and lifetime income that can be generated from the investments. After all, two portfolios could have the same risk score but different returns and future income potential.

Another way of thinking about this process is that you and other investors each have a personalized budget for risk—there is just so much risk that you can afford to take. Each investment has its own risk, so that enters into the equation. But diversifying your mix means having investments whose risks at least partially cancel each other out. This makes riskier investments more affordable for you.

Such an approach is top-down, proactive, and process driven. It removes much of the emotion of investing and moves it closer to being a science. It is different from the bottom-up approach that most people use, accumulating investments one at a time because they look good.

ANNIE WANTS TO USE HER INVESTMENT CLUB EXPERIENCE

Annie has now been in her investment club for a few months, and she and her new friends have picked stocks to invest in. The club's performance has been fine so far, and she has enjoyed the challenges.

Annie believes that she is ready to roll out this approach and start buying stocks for her own account. Is she?

The experience that Annie has gained is helpful, but she still has a couple of major challenges. First, if she purchases stocks of individual companies as she has in the investment club, and not pools of investments, she will have to watch and manage her stocks closely. Even then, she will be competing against professional money managers, who have the tools to react to economic and corporate news in a fraction of a second. She may well decide to switch to using pooled investments, like mutual funds. If she does, she will find it easier to construct a diversified portfolio and achieve more consistent returns.

Second, the investment club approach is to evaluate investments one at a time and add them if they look "good." This approach is used by many, if not most, investors. Annie should learn how to evaluate investment alternatives in part by how effectively they work together and produce the income she will need for her retirement with the risk that she is prepared to take. A professional may be able to help her with this process.

MIXES FOR DIFFERENT PURPOSES

You will probably not want all your money to be invested for the long run, which is usually defined as at least five to ten years. You will want to manage some short-term money differently, for such purposes as bill paying, emergencies, and goals that you need to meet soon. If, for example, you have put together a college fund for a grandchild who will be starting college soon, you do not want to have to ask the grandchild to wait until the stock market returns back to where it has been before you can help out.

Cash is king because of its stability in value and liquidity. You can also use cash substitutes, like money market funds, short-term certificates of deposit, and ultrashort-term bond funds, for the same purposes.

How much cash do you need to have on hand? That is a matter of individual preference, but many retirees have anywhere from a few months' to a few years' worth of expenses in cash or cash-equivalent accounts.

If you need a pool of money to tap in two to five years, then those investments or a mix of investments should have a much lower risk score than your long-term money.

TIMING THE MIX

Just as there are passive investments—with a buy-and-hold approach—there are also passively managed portfolios. Managing your portfolio actively—getting in and out of the market when you believe it is appropriate—is extraordinarily difficult. You must get your timing right many times when you are buying and selling. Even if you sell your riskier investments at a high point, you may have difficulty buying them back at an appropriate time. Then you get locked out of the market when it is rising.

If you insist on timing, you will do better to carve out a small part of your portfolio and actively manage that. It is just too risky to bet the farm with everything you own.

As described in Chapter 13, the research using Monte Carlo modeling on glide patterns shows that making your portfolio more conservative as you age is generally a bad idea.

PREPARING YOUR INVESTMENT MIX FOR RETIREMENT

Reviewing your investment mix is an important task in your preparations for retirement. You can determine fairly quickly if your investments are like the diet of many flavors of only ice cream. If so, you should look for investment ingredients that will diversify it.

You can measure the quality of your investment portfolio as described in this chapter. Does it match the risks that you are prepared to take? Are there other mixes that will work better for you? The answer is not to find the mix with the highest return but instead the one that can generate the highest sustainable income for you.

When you are working with only the limited menu of investment alternatives that is in your current 401(k) or other retirement plans, you will come up with one mix that is optimal. As you take advantage of the wider range of investment choices available in the broader investment world, you should be able to put together better diversified and more effective portfolio mixes that will provide more income for you. That improved portfolio should better weather the inevitable storms of the future.

If the tasks of choosing individual investments, mixing them together to form efficient portfolios, and matching them to your risk profile are more than you can or want to do, get professional help.

A caveat: Don't be too optimistic about future returns based on historic returns. Any analysis you do will help show you what your choices are and what the impacts of those choices may be. No analysis, however, will give you the exact dollar amounts for returns and income. You should rerun analyses again as your situation evolves.

17. Taxes: The Tail That Wags the Dog

Many people mistakenly believe that income taxes will be much less of a problem when they retire. After all, if they are no longer earning a salary, then they will have less to tax. But the reality is that when you turn seventy and a half and start taking your annual required minimum distributions from retirement plans, which are taxable, your taxable income could equal your previous earned income. If your retirement plans are large enough, your income taxes can actually increase. Your income taxes could be your single largest expense in retirement.

Since much of your retirement income may come from your investments, the setup of your investments can have a profound effect on your taxes. Sometimes it seems as if taxes are the tail that wags the (investment) dog, particularly because taxes are a key component of investment planning. During retirement, taxes on investments become a bigger deal for two major reasons:

- Taxes on investments may well be one of your largest expenses in retirement. You will be able to spend only your net investment income, the amount leftover after you have paid taxes. So taxes will have an immediate effect on your lifestyle.

- You frequently have choices about the type of account in which to own an investment, and those choices can have a profound effect on your taxes.

Investment planning in general includes not just choosing the right investments and the right mix of them but also putting the investments in the most advantageous accounts from a tax standpoint. In fact, the major component of "investment strategy" is doing just that. It makes a difference for tax purposes, for example, if an investment is in a personally held account or an IRA.

Is it immoral to contrive to pay lower taxes? One of Judge Learned Hand's famous quotes is, "Over and over again, courts have said that there is nothing sinister in so arranging one's affairs as to keep taxes as low as possible. Everybody does so, rich or poor; and all do right, for nobody owes any public duty to pay more than the law demands: taxes are enforced exactions, not voluntary contributions. To demand more in the name of morals is mere cant."

CAVEAT ON TAX ADVICE
Giving tax advice in print is hazardous for a few key reasons:

- Taxes are complicated—there are tens of thousands of pages of tax laws. They are not meant to be logical. They exist to raise revenue for government programs and promote social policies believed to be in the best interests of people and government.

  Many of the rules have exceptions and details that could affect the application to your particular circumstances. Many of those details are beyond the scope of this book.
- Tax laws are constantly changing from actions of all three branches of government and also taxpayers. Congress and other legislative bodies pass the laws. Afterwards they may try to close "loopholes," which is another term for effective investment strategies that provide unintended benefits for some people. Sometimes even small changes can have big effects.

The Tax Cuts and Jobs Act of 2017 instituted major changes to the tax code. Its implications have yet to be determined, but it will have many unintended consequences, and new investment strategies will be developed.

The executive branch decides which tax laws to enforce and how forcefully. Taxpayers, both individual and corporate, challenge tax laws through varying interpretations. The judicial system at all levels decides how the laws are to be interpreted.

For all of these reasons, you should consult with your tax advisor to keep up with the changes and apply the laws to your particular situation. Nevertheless, having a general understanding of the tax laws is imperative so you can identify and take advantage of investment opportunities.

GENERAL APPROACHES TO REDUCING TAXES

The ideal situation is to eliminate taxes on investments, but, in reality, the best you can do is to postpone them. If you postpone taxes, you get to use the money that will eventually go to the government. The money that you keep, even if only temporarily, will grow and produce more income for you.

There are three different times in the lifetime of holding your investments when you might receive some kind of tax advantage:

- *When you purchase the investment.* Sometimes you are permitted to deduct your investment from your taxable income when you prepare your taxes. If you purchase an investment under your name, you cannot do this. But if you add money to your 401(k) account to purchase the identical investment, you can. This is sometimes called a pretax investment.
- *When you own an investment.* When you own an investment under your name, you pay taxes on interest, dividends, and capital gains as described. But if you own the identical in-

vestment in your 401(k) or other sheltered account, you pay none of these taxes. If you buy or sell investments inside your 401(k), there are no taxes to be paid.

- *When you take a distribution from an investment.* When you sell an investment under your name, you pay taxes on capital gains at the capital gains rate, which is lower than the tax rate on earned income. But if you take any money out of your 401(k), whether there was a gain or not, you must pay taxes on the whole amount withdrawn at your regular income tax rate.

THE BASICS ON TAXES ON INVESTMENTS

Taxes on individual investments. Bonds pay interest or dividends, both of which are taxed like earned income—except when they aren't. The exceptions include interest on U.S. Treasury bonds, bills, and notes, which are subject to federal but not state income tax. Interest from municipal bonds, which are issued by states and municipalities, are not subject to federal income tax but may or may not be subject to state income tax. You do not pay taxes on interest on U.S. savings bonds until you cash them in.

Zero-coupon bonds, which you buy at a discount from their maturation value, pay no interest, but you still must pay tax on their imputed value increase.

Dividends on most individual stocks that you have held for a while, generally a year, are qualified dividends and are taxed at the lower, capital gains rate.

You pay taxes on the appreciation of stocks, real estate, and other securities only when you "realize" those gains, that is, when you sell the security. Thus, you can shelter gains through the years before selling the investment.

The appreciation of value is taxed at the capital gains rate if the security is long-term, that is, has been held for more than a year. If the security has been held for less than a year, the gain is taxed at the regular rate.

If you sell your investment with a loss in value, you can use it to offset your capital gains. If capital losses exceed capital gains, you can deduct up to $3,000 per year of losses against your regular income. You can carry over losses in excess of $3,000 to tax calculations for future years to continue to deduct them from taxable income.

Some individual investments contain special tax deals. For example, drilling for oil may have an oil-depletion allowance, which is an upfront deduction of part of your investment. Investing in Section 8 low-income housing has special advantages. Real estate can have a depreciation allowance, which allows you to deduct money for the wear and tear of the buildings you own.

Taxes on pooled investments. A pooled investment, such as a mutual fund, is a pass-through entity. This means that you are subject to the same taxes on interest, dividends, and capital gains that occur inside the fund for your share of the ownership of the fund, even if you yourself do not sell your fund shares. The fund manager sells securities either as part of the management of the fund or to raise money to pay off other investors who sell their shares. Those sales have capital gains or losses, which affect you directly.

Mutual funds tend to distribute capital gains to fund owners toward the end of the year. Each mutual fund you buy will have embedded capital gains or losses in it, depending on the history of the fund. You should be aware of this so that you are not blindsided when a fund you own has no or even a negative return for the year, yet you end up with a capital gain to pay taxes on because the fund sold some of its past winners.

When you sell shares in your mutual fund, your taxes will be based on your gain, which is the difference between the proceeds you received and the amount you invested, which is your basis. If you have been reinvesting dividends or capital gains paid by the fund, remember that those reinvestments will increase the basis for your fund. If you have not kept a record of all reimbursements, the mutual fund company may have a record that they can send you.

BUCKETS FOR TAX SHELTERING

How they work. You can own investments inside of buckets, that is, different tax entities, such as your trusts, IRAs, limited liability corporations (LLCs), and many others. Each has its own rules, which sometimes supersede the tax rules for an investment you hold in your name. For example, if your IRA contains a mutual fund that has capital gains or dividends, you do not pay taxes. Instead, you pay taxes only when you distribute money from the IRA to you as an individual. All IRA and retirement plan distributions are taxable as regular income no matter how that income was derived.

To make successful decisions about which buckets you should use to minimize taxes, it is critical for you to understand how the buckets work and how to get money into and out of the buckets.

You might want to use some buckets not to provide particular tax advantages but because they will give you a different kind of control over your investments. If you own a business that in turn owns investments, then the type of business entity will determine how your investment or investment income is taxed.

For example, if you own shares in your own C corporation, the corporation must pay its own taxes first, and then you also pay taxes when you receive the income. But a Subchapter S corporation, an LLC, or a partnership will pass the income directly to you as if the bucket does not even exist.

There are different rules for the two major classifications of trusts. A revocable (living) trust permits you to move investments or money into or out of the trust with no tax consequences. It may well use the same tax identification number as you. You, and not the trust, pays taxes.

On the other hand, you can add to an irrevocable trust but distribute money only as a gift to the beneficiaries of the trust according to the terms of the trust. The irrevocable trust pays its own taxes at higher rates than you would. Be aware that if all owners of a revocable trust die and the trust now holds assets for the estate, the revocable trust automatically becomes irrevocable and is taxed differently.

Your retirement plan at your place of employment is a bucket that permits you to purchase investments on a pretax basis. You sign an agreement permitting your employer to channel some of your pay into the plan. Your employer may or may not match some of your contributions.

There are many variations of retirement plans, many with a number that identifies the section of the tax code that permits it—a 401(k), 403(b), 457, money-purchase plan, Keogh, SIMPLE IRA, Simplified Employee Pension (SEP), and others.

Once money is in the retirement plan, it grows or shrinks depending on the investments that you have chosen and their performance. Interest, dividends, and capital gains are not taxable, and you receive no 1099 tax form, unless or until you distribute money from the retirement plan. All distributions are then subject to tax at your regular rate.

The retirement plan provides two huge advantages over saving money after you have received it as wages. First, saving money by putting it into the retirement plan is easier because money that would have been paid in taxes goes into your plan and you get to have it grow in your account. Second, you save tax money through tax deferral all those years before you take out money.

You can also set up your own Individual Retirement Account (IRA). If you have an adjusted gross income lower than $119,000 (married, or $72,000 single) or no retirement plan at work, you can contribute on a pretax basis, that is, you get to deduct IRA contributions from your taxable income. If your income is higher than these thresholds and you have a retirement plan, you will not get the IRA deduction from your taxable income. You will be able to contribute to the IRA, and your income inside the IRA will be tax deferred until you distribute it.

Many employers will require you to leave your retirement plan where it is while you are working. But you can take your money out after you leave so that you can achieve more diversification than the work retirement plan provides. You can maintain the tax-favored nature of your retirement money by transferring it directly into an IRA that you have set up to receive it. This is called an IRA rollover.

Whether you receive the money yourself or transfer it to your rollover IRA, you will receive a 1099 tax form after the end of the year showing the distribution of the money to you. You must declare it as having been received, but you do not have to pay taxes on the distribution if it has been transferred properly to your IRA.

You can transfer multiple retirement plans to the same IRA if you like. And you can transfer one IRA to another by a process called a 1035 exchange. Make sure that you do not receive the money yourself if you want to have the maximum flexibility in managing the accounts.

BRIAN CONSOLIDATES HIS RETIREMENT PLANS

Brian is no longer working at his sales job. He realizes that at some point he will need to do something with his retirement plan at work in order to generate the income he will need in retirement. He had a number of other sales jobs when he was in his twenties, thirties, and forties. He has not been receiving retirement plan statements from any of his previous employers. He wonders if he might be entitled to other retirement benefits and how to proceed.

Brian needs to set up his own IRA into which he can transfer the investments or cash from his retirement plan at his recent job. Then he transfers his retirement plan money into his new IRA. Next Brian should contact the benefits departments from each of his previous employers to learn about what he may be entitled to, if any.

Some former employers will accept transfer paperwork associated with his new IRA. Other employers might require that Brian use their own paperwork for the transfer. In all cases, the money should go directly into Brian's own IRA, and not directly to Brian, to avoid taxes on the distributions.

Buckets with a tax advantage upon distribution. A Roth IRA, a Roth SIMPLE IRA, and a Roth 401(k) all permit contributing to an account with after-tax money, that is, no upfront tax break. The account grows tax deferred like a retirement account or IRA. The advantage of a Roth is that distributions from contributions to the Roth are not taxed. Growth on the original contributions are not subject to income tax if the Roth is at least five years old.

There is a dollar cap on how much you can contribute to a traditional IRA, a Roth IRA, or both when added together. However, you can convert a traditional IRA to a Roth IRA. This is called a Roth conversion. You do this by setting up your Roth IRA account and transferring money into it from the traditional IRA. Those distributions from the IRA are fully taxable, like other non-1035 distributions, so make sure that you have the money to pay the taxes.

If you are in the same tax bracket when you contribute to an IRA or a Roth as you are when you make distributions, you end up with exactly the same after-tax money from either approach. If your tax bracket is lower when you are retired and distributing money, you will end up with more after-tax money from the Roth, and vice versa.

Cash-value life insurance policies can contain investments, which some people use as a supplemental retirement plan with after-tax contributions. You make contributions to the insurance plan for more than what is needed to pay for the life insurance costs themselves. Those investments grow tax deferred, and if set up properly, there is no tax upon death or lifetime distributions. In this way they act like Roth IRAs. You can borrow the excess contributions and their growth to pay for retirement costs without paying taxes. But you need to have the insurance policy in effect until death, when your beneficiaries receive what is left in the policy tax-free. If the insurance policy runs out of money before you die, there can be large adverse tax consequences. This approach takes careful planning and perfect execution.

Another tax-advantaged bucket. You can own an annuity inside a tax-advantaged bucket, in which case the rule for the bucket supersedes the rules of the annuity. You might own the annuity not for its tax benefit but for the lifetime guarantees or death benefits—the special features of the annuity.

If you own an annuity not in a retirement plan, then you get no tax break when you contribute to or take distributions from it. But you do get tax deferral on interest, dividends, and capital gains while the funds remain in the annuity. You generally are required to take gains out before the principal investment and pay taxes at your regular rate then.

Annuities can have different owners (who make the decisions), annuitants (whose death triggers a payout to beneficiaries) and beneficiaries (who collect upon death). Be careful, because there could be unintended tax consequences from setting it up improperly. The laws differ from state to state and depend on the specific provisions of the annuity contract. Work with a financial professional when setting it up.

INVESTMENT STRATEGIES

A number of strategies are available to reduce your taxes. Here are a few that have survived recent changes to the tax laws.

Put the right investments in the right buckets. The first two steps in the construction of your investment portfolio are identifying the right investments to include and then deciding the appropriate mix of those investments based in part on the risks that you are prepared to take.

The third is to decide what goes where. You will most likely own a mix of investments and a mix of accounts. Those accounts will be categorized as either qualified to get a tax break, like 401(k)s and traditional and Roth IRAs, or nonqualified, like personal accounts. Your investment mix will contain higher-return but more volatile capital gains–oriented investments, like stocks, and lower-return income-oriented investments, like bonds and cash.

In general, you will be better off sheltering the more highly taxed investments, like bonds, inside your qualified accounts. You will be able to defer paying taxes on them until you cash them out and take distributions.

If you are using a buy-and-hold approach with your stocks through owning individual securities or passively invested stock mutual funds, including index funds, then most of your returns will be sheltered from taxation even in your nonqualified accounts. When you do cash in your stocks, you will pay taxes at the capital gains tax rate. Some of your dividends, those that are qualified to get a tax break, will not be taxed.

These tax breaks will be lost if your stocks are held inside your qualified accounts. All interest, dividends, principal, and capital gains will be taxed at your regular tax rate when distributed, because all distributions—principal and growth—are taxed.

Furthermore, your qualified accounts holding bonds will grow at a slower rate than if they had stocks in them. Smaller IRAs will require smaller required minimum distributions (see below) and associated income taxes.

You may want some of your cash in either qualified or nonqualified accounts. Cash is an excellent source of funding for emergencies and income to live off. So whatever bucket you will be taking distributions from to pay for your lifestyle should hold your cash.

Because dividends, interest, and capital gains on investments in your Roth IRA will never be taxed, you can store any kind of investments there.

Shelter the front- and back-door ways. If you are still earning money and in a savings mode, make sure to shelter your investments from taxes as much as possible. You do this by setting up a variety of tax-advantaged buckets and channeling as much of your savings as possible into those buckets. You should also choose some investments that are tax-advantaged themselves. This approach is the direct front-door way to shelter money in investments as it is earned.

Some people receive a lump sum of money, most frequently from an inheritance. You can shelter this money using a few approaches.

The first is to invest the money in an annuity. The annuity will have no up-front or distribution tax benefits, but investments in the annuity will grow tax deferred until distributed.

A second approach is available if you are still working and not contributing the maximum amount to your retirement plan. Then you use the money to increase your contribution to the maximum possible. This approach has two results: more money ends up being sheltered, and you get a tax break from the larger contribution to the retirement plan.

If you find yourself running short of money to pay for your expenses, then you can make up the difference by using small amounts of your lump sum. The tax break permits you to use a smaller proportion of the lump sum than you might have thought.

A third approach is to set up and contribute some of the lump sum to a charitable remainder trust (CRT). You receive an up-front partial tax deduction for the contribution, and income inside the CRT is not taxed until distributed, if set up to accomplish that. The CRT limits the size of the permitted distributions, although distributions not taken in any year can be taken out later if the CRT is set up appropriately. The CRT has a finite lifetime, perhaps yours and your partners, and sometimes more than that. When the time is up, any money remaining in the CRT goes to charities of your choice. This approach works especially well if you are planning to leave money to charities anyway.

Sell investments in the right ways. Sometimes you may want to sell or change investments inside a tax-advantaged account. You can do that without incurring any taxes. But if you need to take money out of the account, you must do that carefully. The most effective way of accomplishing that is to do a tax-free transfer by rolling your IRA over to another IRA. This process is the same as rolling over a retirement plan into an IRA and is a way to consolidate retirement plans from multiple jobs and careers.

You can also do a 1035 exchange from one life insurance policy to another, more appropriate policy. Or you can exchange the life insurance for an annuity so that you can keep the money invested without having to continue paying premiums. You can also do a 1035 exchange from an annuity to an annuity, or from an annuity or life insurance policy to a long-term care insurance plan without paying taxes on any gain. These 1035 exchanges postpone paying taxes on any gains above the amount invested, which would have to be paid if they were just cashed in.

You can also use a 1031 exchange to sell one piece of real estate and purchase another while postponing any taxes on capital gains. The rules for a 1031 exchange are much more complicated than for a 1035 exchange but in the right circumstances can be done.

Manage cash flows in the different phases of your retirement. At this point you may view your upcoming retirement as having different phases not just based on your changing health but on the activities you undertake.

From the financial and tax standpoints, three common milestone events can occur that will affect your taxes. One is retirement itself, when you stop working, the second is when you start collecting Social Security, and the third is the onset of your required minimum distributions (RMDs) from IRAs and some other retirement plans. You may or may not have a substantial interval between one or more of these milestones.

Social Security generally starts between ages sixty-two and seventy, but with careful planning you may also collect a smaller, spousal benefit before collecting your own benefit (see Chapter 14.)

RMDs start in the year you turn seventy and a half. You can postpone taking an RMD up until April 1 of the following year, but then you will need to take out both years of distributions during that calendar year. You can postpone taking distributions only from the retirement plan of the place you are currently working if you are over seventy and a half and own less than 5 percent of the firm.

You calculate the amount of the RMD from the value of all qualified plans on the previous December 31 divided by an IRS distribution period for your age at the following December 31. For example, the distribution periods at ages seventy, eighty, ninety, and one hundred are 27.4, 18.7, 11.4, and 6.3, respectively. So at age seventy your IRA containing $100,000 requires an RMD of $100,000/27.4 = $3,649.64. If you have multiple IRAs, you can take the RMD from one or more of them. RMDs from 401(k) plans need to be calculated and distributed separately.

If you have more than $100,000 in IRAs and qualified plans, then you must distribute correspondingly more, whether you need the money or not. The RMD was set up to require qualified plan holders to start paying taxes on retirement fund savings.

After age seventy and a half, you may not need the RMD money to live off. If so, then your tax burden is higher than you want and need. So tax planning involves reducing the amount of the RMDs.

You could have a year or more when your taxable income is relatively low, depending on when your milestones occur. Capital gains tax rates under current law can be 0 percent, 15 percent, or 20 percent, depending on your adjusted gross income including the capital gains. If you realize those capital gains in a low-income year, you may then be able to avoid some or all of the taxes on your capital gains.

Permanently lower your taxes on RMDs. RMDs are calculated based on your total amount of retirement plans and IRAs, but not Roth IRAs. So to decrease the amount of both you can simply cash them in. This is not a good strategy, because you will have to pay taxes on the amount cashed in and the remaining funds will not be sheltered.

A much better alternative is to convert IRAs to Roth IRAs. Taxes will still need to be paid, but the resulting funds will be sheltered from taxes forever, partly because there are no RMDs on Roth IRAs until your death. Roth IRAs pass income tax–free to your beneficiaries when received.

You can use any nonqualified money that you already have—investments in your name or after-tax income—to pay the taxes for the Roth conversion. You will end up with the same amount of money sheltered as you had in the IRAs, but taxes will never be due. So you have improved the quality of the sheltered account. It is equivalent to another back-door approach to sheltering either your income or investments. In either case—funding with qualified or nonqualified money—your RMDs will decrease permanently.

Part of your planning for Roth conversions must include putting money aside to pay the extra taxes. If you do the conversions at times when your income is lower, then you will be in a lower tax bracket than if you do the whole conversion at once. This is a reason for doing Roth conversions gradually over time.

When you are deciding between having traditional IRAs or Roth IRAs in your portfolio, you may be thinking that a critical factor is the tax rate when you have to pay taxes. For example, if tax rates are high when you are young, then you will do better to contribute to a pretax IRA and get the deduction then, rather than taking money from the plan when taxes are low. However, you do not know what future tax rates will be. You can even argue that having a mix of traditional and Roth IRAs is a way to diversify your portfolio against the ups and downs from changes in the tax laws.

BRIAN AND BECKY PLAN FOR THEIR INVESTMENT TAXES

Taxes have always been a background issue for Brian and Becky. Long ago they decided not to do taxes themselves but to gather their paperwork into a large paper bag and bring it to the local office of a large chain of tax preparers. They are confident that their preparer has done a good job of calculating what they have needed to pay.

Now that they are thinking more about retiring and living off Becky's pension and their investments, they are wondering about tax planning. To them, this means not just looking backward over the past year but planning for the future. Maybe they can do a better job of lowering their taxes. They are concerned about making ends meet and want to make sure that their after-tax money will be as high as it can be. And maybe their taxes will get more complicated if Brian starts a consulting business.

Accountants are trained to do an excellent job of calculating the minimum taxes that you have to pay on last year's income. Generally, they are not experts on investments and investment planning. An investment or financial planner will have more expertise in these areas. The best approach is to work with both tax and investment professionals as a team.

If Brian gets serious about starting a consulting business, he should work with an accountant who has experience working with small-business owners.

PREPARING FOR INVESTMENT TAXES IN RETIREMENT

If you have some time before your retirement, your highest priority should be on those issues that take some time to accomplish. One is to continue building your retirement accounts through as automatic savings as possible. You will be most effective by contributing to tax-advantaged accounts wherever possible.

Your other high priority approach should be to start your Roth conversions early so that you can do them gradually without being pushed into a higher tax bracket.

You should also be planning to take full advantage of your tax brackets, for example by selling appreciated investments when your capital gains tax brackets are lower.

You can improve the quality of your investment portfolio at any time, before or after your retirement. This means choosing lower cost and higher quality individual investments and changing the mix of your investments to better match the liquidity you need and the risks you are prepared to take. Doing this sooner will work better for you in the long run.

18. Planning Anyhow

Many people ridicule the whole idea of planning. They may say that "man plans and God laughs." Or "The best military plans work until the first shot is fired." Yes, plans generally do not work exactly as expected, but they can help you in a variety of ways, particularly in dealing with complicated issues, by getting you to think them through and to ask for feedback on your ideas.

As you get serious about retiring, you will have a lot to think about and will have many decisions to make in a whole range of areas. Decisions in one area may well have consequences in others. How do you put all of the ideas together so that you can take action effectively? The answer is through systematic planning and the construction of a written financial plan.

The purpose of a financial or any other plan is to spell out the steps you need to take to accomplish your objectives. Detailed plans are particularly important if a project or set of action steps is complicated because it has many steps to be completed over a long time period. A written plan:

- reminds you what you need to do and keeps you on track,
- allows you to share the plan and get feedback from others, and
- instructs others about what needs to be done.

A review of a written plan will lead to more thoughtful and helpful feedback from others.

You do not have to have a written plan for every little task that you want to accomplish—a prioritized task list will work better for that. If you have in mind a large project with many steps, you can focus your actions on the first few steps that need to be accomplished, and put the later steps on a reserve list to refer to later.

The benefits of a well-thought-out plan can be substantial. A well-thought-out and executed plan can help you achieve a more amazing life. If you have important goals to achieve, the plan will spell them out and help you achieve them. You can consciously orient your plan around your values to have a more values-focused life. It will help you put your resources—time, money, and energy—to their best possible uses. You will focus more on what is possible and have more to show for your time.

Before you make the transition to retirement, you should have in place two planning documents: a financial plan and an investment policy statement. The first of these provides a road map for you and your finances. The second is a guideline for setting up, managing, and using your investments on a routine basis.

You do not need to wait for retirement to put these documents in place. You can develop them at any time and modify them as needed in the future.

THE FINANCIAL PLAN

A financial plan is generally developed as a collaborative process with a professional who has the expertise and the objectivity to provide the necessary insights. A Certified Financial Planner (CFP) is an excellent candidate to serve in that role. A CFP has professional training and certification in the area. The CFP is required to be objective and use a fiduciary standard, that is, to make recommendations that are in your interests first, before his or her own.

A financial plan is a written blueprint for how to proceed with your next steps in life. Its written form can vary depending on the topics covered and the author of the plan. Its scope—the areas planned for—can vary widely. Its common core includes budgeting and projections, as discussed in Chapter 11, a discussion of and recommendations for investments, and retirement. It will frequently include many of these additional financial topics: insurance of many kinds, estate planning, tax issues, employee benefits, and support and/or education for other family members—children, grandchildren, and parents.

Financial planning is a process. Its process and rhythm are similar to that of other professions, such as law and medicine. Here are its six steps:

1. *Define and establish a working relationship.* Here you define the scope of your work together with the financial planner—topics to be reviewed and costs. You both sign a formal contract to get the work done.

2. *Gather data and goal information.* The materials you need to assemble can be substantial, depending on the scope of your agreement. These can include investment, savings, and insurance statements of all kinds; legal agreements; benefit statements if still working; budgeting information; and tax returns. You and the planner will probably have extensive and in-depth discussion of your personal and family histories and your hopes and dreams for the future.

3. *Analyze and evaluate the current situation.* Questions and computer software are the main tools for gaining insights. The planner may develop computer models to describe how your current financial situation works.

4. *Develop and present alternatives and recommendations.* This stage can have a substantial educational component, because there may be ideas that you are not familiar with. This is

when the "what ifs" are developed so that you can try out different ideas for how to proceed.

5. *Implement recommendations.* Your financial planner may have the capabilities to do much of the implementation but may need to pull in other specialists, such as an accountant or an attorney among others, to make their contributions. It can take months or occasionally even years to act on all of the recommendations.

6. *Monitor recommendations.* This phase implies a continuing working relationship with your financial planner. You can then make adjustments to your plan as needed because of changes in the economy and in your goals, family, health, community, and finances.

This in-depth financial planning should give you the perspective to make the critical decisions for your future retirement.

The most in-depth financial planning is sometimes called life planning. It includes the financial aspects of attaining dreams and goals, establishing meaning in your life, and planning charitable giving. The boundaries between financial and life planning can be fuzzy, because financial planning itself might contain these topics, depending on the scope of the financial planning contract. Both take into account your special situation and changes in family issues, including marital status or (grand)parenthood, health, employment, and others.

Here are two hints for writing and using your financial plan:

- Shorter is better. A professional financial plan can be fifty or more pages long. If so, make sure that it contains a summary. You are more likely to routinely use the summary as a living, breathing document.

- Discuss your financial plan with others. Other people, such as other professionals or close family members, can help you improve the quality of your document and planning and even be accountability partners and coaches to make sure that your document is not just put on a shelf to gather dust.

THE INVESTMENT POLICY STATEMENT

Organizations and their boards of directors that have the responsibility of managing the investments of their organizations have traditionally been the main users of the investment policy statement (IPS). Because they are responsible for other people's money, they are held to a high fiduciary standard. In fact, they can be held personally liable if they have not acted professionally and prudently in their investment planning. They meet that responsibility by creating and using an IPS.

Although 50 percent of all organizations with money to manage, both for-profit and nonprofit, use an IPS to administer their investments, only 2 percent of individuals, who in general and on average are less successful than professionals, have them.

CATHY CONSTRUCTS HER OWN IPS
TO MANAGE HER INVESTMENTS

Cathy has been thinking for a while about coordinating the three transitions she and Chuck are going through: the growth of their restaurant business, the transition of ownership from Cathy and Chuck to Courtney, and the transition to living off their investments in retirement. Regarding the investment part of this, Chuck's attitude is, "whatever." So Cathy has been the one doing the reading and research about how investments really work. She stumbled on the Dalbar research that shows that individual investors substantially underperform professional money managers. Cathy wonders why and how professional investors are more successful and what she and Chuck can do to have a better experience of investing before and during their retirement years.

To sort this all out, Cathy and Chuck need to go through the financial planning process first and develop a financial plan for the transitions. They should hire a financial planner with special expertise in planning for businesses, because their issues are more complex and require specialized knowledge and tools.

For the management of their investment portfolio, Cathy and Chuck should work with an investment or financial planner to create an IPS. Here is what their IPS document should contain:

Lifestyle goals. These goals specify how Cathy and Chuck plan to use their money. They might list financial independence over their lifetimes as one of them. They would then spell out how long their money needs to last and determine the probability of meeting this goal (e.g., 95 percent chance of lasting until age ninety-five). They should also list their lifestyle goals, such as time with family, a variety of activities to be enjoyed, and family and community organizations to be supported during their lifetime as appropriate. They can be as specific as they like.

Legacy goals. Since their lifetimes are finite, the IPS spells out what is to happen to their investment money when they are finished using it.

General investment considerations. These include
- the risks that they are prepared to take with their investments. Their risk score would work best here because it is measurable.
- their use of tax-advantaged accounts
- their unique needs and circumstance, for example, the role of their business, involvement of family members, and so on
- the people responsible for carrying out the instructions in the IPS

Asset allocation strategy
- liquidity requirements, that is, how much money should be in cash and where it is stored
- asset classes included in the portfolio

- restrictions on assets or asset classes so that they are not included in the portfolio

Investment management
- the frequency for reviewing investments
- the people with that responsibility
- the criteria for making changes

Cash flow
- all expected sources of income and amounts
- all large, elective anticipated expenses, for example, for support of family members, gifting, travel, charitable contributions, and others

THE CASH AND INVESTMENT POLICY STATEMENT

The Cash and Investment Policy Statement (CIPS) contains all of the information in the IPS plus a section that summarizes your present and possible future cash flows. You obtain the numbers from your budgeting. (See Chapter 11.)

The CIPS briefly lists your sources of income, such as Social Security, pensions, annuities, and investments. If you are or will be living off your investments, you can estimate your investment income as 4 percent of your investment portfolio value (see Chapter 13). If you are working for pay, include that as well.

Your summary of expenses should be even briefer. It might include just items for routine small and large ongoing expenses. If your income is greater than your expenses, the difference will be savings / discretionary spending.

If you are close to a major transition in your financial life, such as retirement, your CIPS can show the difference between cash flow before and after the transition.

You should have an IPS or a CIPS for a number of reasons:

- First, your investment portfolio will probably have better returns and ultimately more income. Writing everything down will make it much easier to evaluate your whole approach and get feedback from others to improve on your original ideas. You will have a better sense of how your investments will work together.

- Second, you will manage your investments much better. You will make better ongoing decisions because you will have your criteria for changes all spelled out. This will permit you to act more rationally and take many of the destructive emotions out of the picture—overconfidence, overreliance on the familiar, and motivation by fear and greed, among others. You will be more likely to give the right amount of attention to your investments—not too much and not too little. Because you have spelled out the uses of your investments, you will find it easier to evaluate alternatives for investing and spending. This will help you focus on the right things for you.
- Third, being on top of your investments will help you feel better about them, giving you peace of mind in this area.
- Fourth, if for some reason you do not have a financial plan, an IPS is a good place to start planning your life. It is less complicated than a full-blown financial plan. It can serve as a model for planning other areas of your life—thinking the issues through, writing them down, getting feedback, refining your ideas, and then monitoring regularly.
- Fifth, if you develop a CIPS, you have an easily accessible overview of your cash flow, so that you are clear that you have enough to make ends meet.

Here are two hints for writing and using your IPS or CIPS. They are similar to the hints for a financial plan: shorter is better (two or three pages should be sufficient), and discuss your IPS or CIPS with your partner and possibly others.

PREPARING FOR RETIREMENT PLANNING

To deal with the complexity of your present and future investments and investment income, you will need to construct or update both your financial plan and investment policy statement.

The first step is to get organized, which means taking an inventory of what you have. Here is what you need to assemble:

- personal investment information, including a complete set of recent investment statements
- work information, including
  - pay stub
  - retirement plan and pension statements
  - group life insurance
  - group long-term disability insurance
  - stock options
- personally owned business information
  - product or service
  - percent ownership
  - corporate status
  - original investment
  - current value
- cash flow information, which will serve as the basis for your budgeting, including
  - income statements in addition to work
  - list of expenses
- tax returns from the past two years
- legal documents, including for estate planning
  - wills
  - trusts of all kinds
  - powers of attorney
- insurance policies, including
  - personal life
  - personal long-term disability
  - long-term care
- real estate, including home
  - location
  - purchase date and price
  - current value
  - mortgage information
- vehicles (cars, boats, etc.) and personal property information

- owners
- values
- loans (amounts, completion)
- liabilities (owners and balances)
  - credit cards
  - personal loans
  - student loans
- professional advisors (names, firms, specialties, last time seen)
  - attorneys
  - accountant
  - life insurance agents
  - investment advisers
  - others

Having all of this information assembled will be valuable to you and, more importantly, to anyone who would need to take over for you if you were no longer able to manage your financial affairs by yourself.

After you have assembled this information, you should review

- what information you have and what is missing, and
- the contents of each of these categories, for example, what investments you own.

As a result of this review, you will probably want to

- compose a list of questions about how some of the components of your financial life actually work, and
- formulate tasks to get a better handle on some of these financial areas.

When you have reached this point, you will have more order in your financial life. You will also be prepared to work on and improve your financial situation.

PART THREE

Making It Work

The array and complexity of alternatives in preparing for retirement can be overwhelming. You may get stuck in putting it all together, especially because you may not have the experience to understand the choices and their implications. This part discusses approaches you can use to manage the process of retiring.

19. Getting Help

As you think through what you want to do in retirement and how to prepare for it, you will have many ideas about how to proceed. For some of those ideas, you will know what to do and how to do it. You will find the time to make progress, and the progress will go smoothly. Working to make changes will bring you joy. Everything will come together.

BEING STUCK

Other changes may be more difficult. You might have trouble beginning or following through with the tasks. You might find yourself saying you "should" do this or you "want" to do that, but you make no progress.

The usual reasons that people give for being stuck is that they do not have enough time, knowledge, or experience to do things right. Saying that you have no time really means that right now other activities are more important to you. Maybe you have too much going on now, and now is not the right time. But if these activities are important enough, you will find a way to schedule them into your normal routine.

When people say that they do not have enough experience, they may mean that they don't know what to do or fear doing it all wrong. Getting it right is a challenge for a number of reasons:

- You are not exactly sure what you want to do in retirement. So, how can you prepare for the activities? There are too many possibilities.
- You are not sure how your unique situation and goals affect the decisions you need to make. So finding out what has worked for someone else may or may not be relevant for you.
- You have never retired before. You have only limited experience in many of the decision areas to consider.
- You may be missing critical information that you need to make informed decisions, but to collect that information will take a variety of skills and time, which is scarce.
- You don't know what you don't know. Yet you still have to make decisions. This "not knowing" may be your biggest challenge. Maybe you will find better alternatives later on and make the necessary changes; maybe not. It is not clear which is worse: to find out later about mistakes that are too late to fix, or to live in ignorance!

GETTING UNSTUCK

If you are stuck, getting unstuck may not happen on its own. There is inertia: things go on as they have been unless you apply energy to make a change. Otherwise, same old, same old. And there is entropy: things go downhill unless you apply some combination of time, money, and energy to fix them.

The fear of making mistakes can be a powerful force holding you back. There are two major antidotes to making mistakes. One is to learn from the experiences of others. The other is to use research reports. The essence of research is the systematic analysis of choices and their outcomes. The subjects covered by research are generally more narrowly defined than everyday experience but presumably more reliable. Research is the tool of choice in science and medicine but is used in many other fields as well, including personal finance.

Why not get help? If you really do not have the time to make progress on your own, perhaps you can delegate to or share some of the work with someone else—and tap into their expertise. Using the experience and research of others can increase substantially the quality of your decision making. You will

- understand the scope of your issues—how they fit into your big picture. You may find yourself asking bigger questions about fundamental issues.
- have more clarity, communicate more intelligently, understand the essence of the issues, and fit them into larger concerns.

Getting it right for retirement is important—your outcomes will be better. For example, without proper attention, you might not set up your investments as they should be or file for Social Security benefits at the right time. Then you would live with substantially less income in retirement than is necessary. Or you might miss opportunities for where you live and what you do that would improve your health and energy.

INFORMATION SOURCES AND LEARNING STYLES

If you decide to do your own research, you should take your learning style into account. Perhaps you are an auditory learner—you learn most easily by listening to other people. Radio, television, and books on tape can be good sources of information, if the speaker has appropriate expertise.

Many people check in first with friends and relatives who have navigated similar issues. While their experiences may help you clarify what questions you want to address, rarely do those people have the breadth of experience to provide you with meaningful perspective. Their situations are frequently different from yours and not necessarily relevant.

If you are a visual learner, like most people, then magazines and books can help you, depending on the expertise of the authors. These days, the internet is the go-to place because of the extensive and accessible information that is available there. However, you will find much conflicting and often self-serving information on the internet.

The newest trend for finding pertinent information over the internet is to tap artificial intelligence through robo-advisors. These are computer applications, free or paid, that respond to your entries about your circumstances. The robo-advisor will advise you on how to proceed.

These auditory and visual information resources have advantages. For example, they are free or low cost to use. They are quick. You may have access to information from famous or knowledgeable people that you would not have the opportunity to meet in person. They may call attention to items you need to address.

They also have limitations, however. The responses may be overly simplified, self-serving, contradictory, or impersonal. You may feel that you need still more information. Even after gathering information this way, you may not be sure about what to do next.

VALUE OF PERSONAL HELP

Here are two questions to ask about getting help:

- Will the help make a difference?
- How do you quantify the value of the help, especially if it is intangible?

Consider health planning. You get professional help from your physician when you have a medical condition that needs to be resolved. Yet what about getting help from a personal trainer or dietician/nutritionist, when the benefits may be less immediate but possibly important for your well-being and quality of life? How would you quantify the value of a longer, healthier, or more meaningful life? Do you need to quantify that value?

Consider financial expertise, about which consumers are more skeptical. That help can also be beneficial. This area is more quantifiable because it is in part about money, which can be measured.

Vanguard and Morningstar conducted research studies to measure the monetary value of proper financial planning in overcoming investors' knowledge gaps during retirement. They concluded that the areas of largest deficiencies for investors are the following, in descending order:

- not properly setting up and routinely monitoring investments for income withdrawals during retirement
- not properly allocating and diversifying investments
- not coordinating cash flow with personal goals
- insufficient use of annuities

According to the studies, these four deficiencies together reduce possible retirement income by an estimated 22 percent annually. If you are not set up properly in these areas, you may suffer a substantial impairment of your lifestyle and quality of life.

The case for getting quality help, in spite of the costs, is substantial when you couple these tangible benefits with the intangible ones, such as a feeling of security. That support can help overcome gaps in knowledge and experience.

PARTNERS

Partners work with you on a common goal. There are two kinds of partners: personal and professional. The personal partner does not charge for helping you. Perhaps you have a special connection with a financial coach who is a friend or relative. Or perhaps you have something in common, such as a situation (e.g., about to retire), interest (e.g., exercise), or goal (e.g., changing the world in a particular way). Professional partners are for hire. You might hire them because of their training, expertise, and experience.

Your interactions with both personal and professional partners have many helpful things in common:

- Both types of partner can help you carry some of your load. Together you form a team. You can split up the work based in part on your talents, skills, experience, and interests. Sharing the work can alleviate the "no time" or "no interest" feelings.
- Partners will ask you questions that encourage you to think about your situation in different ways. Those questions will help you clarify your circumstances, including your needs, wants, and feelings. The questions may raise new areas of concern and even offer new possibilities for resolving them.
- Partners may motivate you by caring about the results of your work and by interacting with and encouraging you.
- Partners may hold you accountable for what you say you are going to do. The innocent (or not so innocent) question, How did it go? can challenge you to accomplish your objectives or face the embarrassment of not having made progress. Accountability can include brainstorming to identify and overcome obstacles along the way. You can work together on developing a written plan of action. That plan can become another accountability tool to keep you on track in the future.

PROFESSIONAL PARTNERS

Professional partners come in many kinds. They work with particular bodies of knowledge, for example, accounting and tax laws. They may work with a group of clients of similar age or circumstances, for example, widows. Attorneys may have specialties in estate planning, elder law, business succession, real estate, and other areas. Partners in the financial area can include brokers/registered representatives for securities, insurance agents specializing in different types of insurance policies, and financial planners.

Most professional partners are eager to help you. After all, they are paid for their service work. If they are especially good at what they do, they derive a sense of accomplishment from having a positive impact on the lives of others. Their work may well be their passion.

If they have been in business for a while working with people whose issues are similar to yours, then the experience they have accumulated will provide perspective and insights for you. They will be familiar with and have access to resources, tools, and information of all kinds. They will know the current research, including its methodology, results, limitations, and conclusions.

Their experience can directly benefit you. They will help you identify your core issues by asking the right questions. They will show you alternative courses of action and their consequences.

Professionals can be just as helpful in retirement or preparing for it as they can be at earlier stages of life. No matter when you engage them, professionals will give you advice about how and what to change to improve your situation. Getting help may take some courage, because your professional partner may lead you in new directions out of your comfort zone.

Partners are not just for beginners. Keep in mind that even the best in many fields, including business, entertainment, and sports, hire professional partners or coaches to help them improve their "game" and achieve their goals.

COSTS FOR PROFESSIONAL PARTNERS

The costs for hiring a partner depend on a variety of factors, including their area of specialization, training, level of expertise, responsibilities, time involved, and maybe even the value they provide. Sometimes more work is required for a project than you might think, so the costs can be correspondingly higher.

Partners charge for their services in a wide range of ways: a subscription or flat fees, onetime commissions based on the purchase of products, ongoing fees based on the complexity of work done or responsibilities of the partner, hourly fees, transaction costs, and others. Generally each profession has its preferred way of being compensated for the work done. Each of these methods has its own advantages and disadvantages; any of them can work well or be abused, depending on the integrity of the partner.

CHOOSING THE RIGHT PARTNER FOR YOU

Referrals from other people who have used the same service can be a reliable approach for choosing a service provider. There are even computer services that collect and rate other people's experiences with providers. This approach can be effective for evaluating some service providers. But if the expertise being provided is technical and the consumer has no basis of comparison to make an informed judgment, the value of the evaluation may be hard to assess.

Probably the most useful guide for evaluating technical competence is reputation among and recognition of exemplary performance by an expert's peers. A retired professional, for example, who has no stake in your hiring decisions can tell you whom they trust and recommend. In the research area, including financial research, the Nobel Prize is the gold standard of recognition of the quality of the work.

Providers should be educated, particularly if the area is technical. While education by itself will not substitute for experience, it does inform them of the research in the area. Licensing is one approach to ensuring that practitioners have exposure to at least the minimum assumed knowledge in the field.

Even more important is continuing professional education (CPE) in the field of expertise. Ideas and best practices evolve, and you want your partner to know about them. Some fields do a better job than others in this area. CPE for doctors works well overall because of stringent requirements. Attorneys are regulated by licensing entities in their area of specialization, for example, the National Academy of Elder Law Attorneys, and may have advanced degrees in their specialty.

Educational requirements for financial professionals are more problematic. The initial licensing required to sell financial products is fairly rigorous, but CPE is not. Financial professionals are regulated by brokers/dealers, who require them to know about compliance issues so that they do not get into legal trouble. For example, current educational topics may include fiduciary rules, security and privacy laws, money laundering, details about annuities, which are highly regulated, and limitations on advertising and marketing of financial products. New research results may be available but are not required knowledge.

Two of the optional degrees in the financial field are more rigorous. The Certified Financial Planner (CFP) certification is being accepted more and more as the preeminent degree in the financial field. It requires more education and experience to become licensed than most other accreditations. A CFP must have a fiduciary relationship with clients, that is, the client's interests comes first, always. The licensing examination is now as rigorous as the certified public accountant exam. And its CPE is focused on the latest research.

The insurance industry and its products continue to evolve. The optional designation of choice is the Chartered Life Underwriter (CLU). It is the planning equivalent in the insurance area of the CFP.

COMPETENCE OF PARTNERS

You want your professional partner to be competent. Judging competence is more challenging than it appears. Many people judge their doctors, for example, by how nice they are, how easy they are to communicate with. While these attributes are positive elements of a good physician-patient relationship, do you really want a friendly but incompetent surgeon to work on you? Do you want an affable but incompetent attorney to prepare your will? Affability is an important consideration, but should it be your sole criterion for choosing? While good communication and sharing should play second fiddle to competence, they will make your interactions with your professional partner more efficient, effective, and fun.

You want your partner to be a good listener, not just a talker. The partner should demonstrate that she or he understands what you are saying by repeating it back to you. The partner should want to learn a lot about you and your situation before coming to conclusions and making recommendations. The partner should be empathic during the process. The partner should be able to explain the big picture and how your situation fits in.

When you are interviewing a prospective partner, come prepared with many questions to help you evaluate their competence and their experience in working with people in situations similar to yours. In that process you will also learn about their communication style. You will have an intuitive sense, which you should trust, if the working relationship will be effective.

BECKY AND BRIAN FIND A FINANCIAL ADVISOR

Becky and Brian are overwhelmed by the decisions to make about retirement, mostly about how to fit the pieces together. They know the "when" for Becky but not Brian. They remain unsure about Brian continuing to work. They are unsure about what they can really afford, particularly because they are uncertain about where they will live and how they will make it all happen.

Becky and Brian saw an ad for a brokerage firm on television and decided to go there to get some help planning for retirement. Once there they asked to meet with the firm's best planner, and they were introduced to Eric. Eric's office had a cabinet full of trophies—some for best salesperson of the year and some for golf. Eric was suntanned and wore an expensive suit.

Eric told them that he had made a lot of money for his clients and that Becky and Brian had come to the right place. Eric asked few questions and instead told them at length that his ideas were the best and that they should sign over all of their accounts to him so that he could take care of them. Eric told them that his services were free, that there would be only a small fee for trading investments in their account.

Brian and Becky made a polite escape from Eric as quickly as they could. They were confused and discouraged by what had happened but decided to try again. A friend of theirs had had an excellent experience with Paul, an experienced CFP, so they went to meet him. Their experience with Paul was entirely different.

Paul told them right away that he was not sure that he was the best person for them to work with. Paul asked many questions so that he could determine if they could or should work together. Paul wanted to get a sense of how much help they needed, so he asked questions about where they were and where they wanted to be in the financial and other areas.

Paul talked with them about the amount of work it would take to develop a concrete plan for them, and how much Paul would charge for his services. He described how he had used his experience and CFP training to help others like them. Paul brainstormed with Brian and Becky about their expectations and how they might work together. What appealed most to Becky and Brian is that they would be working together to make progress. They hired Paul on the spot.

You, as a client, must be treated with respect in a working relationship with a professional partner. Yes, the professional needs to be paid, but you want your interests to come first. As you discuss the work to be done, you will establish how much of the work the professional will be doing for you and how much you will do yourself.

PREPARING FOR HELP WITH RETIREMENT ISSUES

As you assemble your list of what you want to do in retirement and begin to plan for the transition, consider using partners—people who can give you the help you need. Choosing partners should be one of the earlier steps in your preparation for retirement.

Think of the different areas you will be working on and who

might be able to help you. Not all of your partners need to be professionals. Friends and family might help you with accountability issues or by sharing some of the work and activities. But if you require serious expertise to get unstuck and make progress, then go to a professional. When you meet with a professional, you should end up with a good sense of the cost and benefits of working together so that you can make an informed decision.

20. Your Best Years Yet

A few years into retirement, retirees fall into two groups. The first group says something like, "Work was my life. Now I have no life." The second group says, "These have been the best years of my life." What made all the difference?

Consider the positive aspects of working. These include your steady income, your work colleagues, the day-to-day structure of your time, the sense of a common purpose at the organization, and being valued for your work contributions. Without the work structure in your retirement life, you may or may not have some of the same positive aspects present.

Researchers have asked both working people and retirees to keep a time diary of their activities. They then compared how the two groups used their time. Retirees used their extra time in many ways, but the three largest increases were for

- household chores, including housework, food preparation, gardening, and home management
- a wide range of leisure activities, including watching an extra hour of television each day. The total time spent on TV was

actually half of all leisure activities each day. Other common leisure activities included reading, shopping, socializing, exercising, relaxing, and volunteering.

- sleep and grooming-related activities, including resting, napping, bathing, and dressing. These increased to more than nine hours each day.

If the sum total of your retirement is spending more time on chores, watching television, doing other leisure activities, and sleeping, you may be busy all of the time. But will the busyness provide meaning to your life, more than you had at work?

CONNECTIONS, EXPLORATIONS, CONTRIBUTIONS

If you ask experienced retirees what activities have given them joy, they tend to answer that it is those activities that involved connecting, exploring, and contributing.

- Connecting is more than spending time with others. Connecting means really communicating and helping others. It might be a smile or serious listening or providing emotional support. It might be supporting other people in activities important to them. Connecting can be with family members, friends, acquaintances, and even strangers.

  Dale Carnegie once said, "You can make more friends in two months by becoming interested in other people than you can in two years by trying to get other people interested in you."

  Connecting with others is the result of an attitude. Can you see the good side in other people so that you truly respect them for who they are? Can you share with them what is in your heart and encourage them to do the same with you?

  New connections can occasionally happen on their own if you are in the right environment, or you can work to make them happen. What kinds of activities can you do to create connections? For example, can you turn important but un-loved activities into meaningful ones by sharing them with others you really care about?

- Exploring can include a wide range of recreational activities, including educational courses, travel to new places, and trying something new. What they have in common is learning. Exploring can give you a deeper understanding of the world around you and of who you are. The sense of accomplishment and insights you gain can be exciting and affect you profoundly.

- Contributing is a way to give back and change the world. You can try to change your community, including even your government, to the way you want it to be. Or you can work on the personal level to help the people around you. Money can be a form of leverage in this area, but the time you spend on a worthwhile cause, the changes that you achieve, the people you help may make all the difference for you as well as for the cause.

What will get you up and going in the morning during your retirement? Will it be more of the same? Will it be the connecting, exploring, and contributing that you do? Will it be the Big Idea that you decide to tackle? Will any of these make you feel particularly fulfilled or resonate with something that is in your heart? Discovering your unique passions may help you overcome the routine nature of your life. Without a planned, intentional approach, routine tasks could simply expand to fill all the time available to do them in retirement.

ENOUGH MONEY

Having enough money for retirement is a key concern. Actually, having enough may not be sufficient to take the worry away. Equally important is *knowing* that you have enough. You may have more than an adequate amount of money but still be fearful. When you have been proactive in planning for your future, you will gain a sense of comfort along with a clear sense of self-determination. That should help you to sleep well at night.

Organizing and analyzing your finances are critical if you want to understand their implications for your future lifestyle. Analysis using budgeting, projections, and financial planning will give you the ability to consider choices and opportunities that you have so that you can make better decisions before problems arise.

PLANNING

Planning should be a comprehensive, ongoing process of

- assessing personal circumstances, including strengths and needs,
- understanding what is plausible and desirable, and
- establishing goals and action steps to get from here to there.

You can use informal or formal planning in a wide range of areas to prepare for retirement. The more complex the issue you need to think through, the more important it is to do formal planning.

The steps in formal planning in any area are the same as the ones outlined in Chapter 18 for financial planning, namely

- getting help,
- gathering data and goal information,
- analyzing the current situation,
- developing alternatives,
- implementing decisions from the analysis, and
- then monitoring progress.

A written summary will help you communicate with others and with yourself in the future.

You can use this methodology in many areas. These could include working on your Big Idea, developing a lifelong travel plan, changing your housing arrangement, working on your relationships, estate planning, improving your health, as well as organizing your finances.

For example, if you are thinking of moving to a warmer climate, you will need to gather data, articulate what you want to accomplish, preferably in writing, define the key areas to be addressed, develop a range of alternatives of where to live and how to get there, and develop an implementation plan. You may bring in partners, such as a realtor for housing and others to walk you through the process of moving. If this project is important enough, you might work with an accountability partner to make sure that you get everything done.

PARTNERING

Whether it is finding someone to help you carry the load or providing expertise in an area, working with someone else can make the difference between success and failure in accomplishing what is important to you. Partners can help you prepare for retirement in any of the areas previously discussed. They can do this in part by being accountability partners for you—encouraging you and spurring you on.

THE RIGHT ATTITUDE

Which of your character traits will help you make the changes necessary to move toward the best years of your life?

- a planned approach—thinking ahead
- open-mindedness—considering a wide range of alternatives
- faith, courage, and good self-talk—believing enough for you to try new things in spite of the risks
- a sense of adventure—trying activities that might be a little scary
- a sense of humor—dealing with life's surprises
- a feeling of gratitude for what happens in your life

If you think of retirement only as no longer working, then retirement is primarily about loss—of colleagues, salary, and professional satisfaction. Alternatively, you can think of retirement as a giant red reset button in your life. You get to decide the direction of your life. So go for it. Make your retirement years your best years yet!

INDEX

ACKNOWLEDGMENTS

First there was the manuscript, and I thought I was done. How naïve could I be? It took a dedicated village to create a book from my manuscript.

My wife, Lucy Rose Fischer, who has published four books, has been a supporter and advocate all along the way. She helped me with editing, general management, ideas, and strategy.

I had many readers, all experts in their fields, review the manuscript for wording and content. Thank you to Charlie Bass, Bill Boyes, Peter Cooper, Chris Farrell, Brent Fisher, Judy Frediani, Kate Gregory, Jan Hively, Jim Jaeckels, Ross Kaplan, Lydia Roth-Laube, and Evan Sarzin.

And then I had help from a number of professionals including: Sarah Miniaci for book consulting, Jeniffer Thompson and Kat Endries for construction of my website, Marshall Davis for videos, Sid Konikoff for photographs, Phil Freshman and Mary Keirstead for copy-editing, and Rachel Holscher and Sarah Miner for cover, page layout, and publication management.

Special thanks to Danika Zick Dorame, my business partner, for supporting me and my financial planning practice for nearly 25 years. Thank you to Nou Yang and my other staff and to my friends for your help and encouragement.

Thank you to my clients who taught me about the challenges and opportunities of retiring.

Mark S. Fischer, CFP and MBA, has helped hundreds of people successfully manage the transition to retirement, both in his work as a financial planner with individual clients and through workshops at the University of Minnesota. He is a specialist on retirement planning. In addition to this book, he is co-author of *Mapping Your Retirement*, a workbook.

Made in the USA
Middletown, DE
29 April 2019